"Christopher Momany inspires us through the stories of these complex, diverse, and faithful heirs of John Wesley—people who witnessed to and embodied love, power, and justice. Through their witness we see that these core values are still needed to keep us 'upright' in a 'world that is downright lost.'"

—**M. Kathryn Armistead**, managing editor, *Methodist Review*

"Remembering that history is story, *Compelling Lives* weaves together overlooked narratives of the American Methodist movement. In this telling, a biblical strand of life and faith is knotted with the impact of the Wesleyan revival on five individuals. Christopher Momany points readers to practices of holiness that call us to a new life in Christ, bringing reconciliation across still-existing human social divides."

—**Joy J. Moore**, professor of biblical preaching, Luther Seminary

"We find here the stories of five compelling lives, compelling not only for the courageous advocacy displayed but also for the ideas which grounded and motivated their abolitionist activity, ideas rooted in faith and philosophy. These lives not only draw us in and hold our attention; they invite self-reflection. How might we embody ideas about human dignity in our own time? This book about compelling lives is itself compelling."

—**David A. Bard**, bishop, Michigan Conference of The United Methodist Church

"A must-read for ministers, religious scholars, students of history, and others genuinely interested in studying models of effective antiracist work. Christopher Momany uses the lives of five Methodist abolitionists to demonstrate how they lived and *practiced* biblical ideals about higher law and natural rights and made them a centerpiece of their antislavery activism. At a time when so many are using Christianity to justify and reinforce division and hate, this is a timely message about its capacity to positively transform humanity."

—**Nikki Taylor**, professor of history, Howard University

D1596427

"In an evangelical Christian world that is running away from the idea of wokeness, particularly in the context of the twenty-first-century rise of white Christian nationalism, it is refreshing to read Christopher Momany's interpretation of the lives of five nineteenth-century radical abolitionists of the Methodist persuasion. Momany skillfully weaves the theological, philosophical, and biblical ideas that lead each of these individuals to 'think, feel and act' in sacrificial ways as advocates of both Christ's freedom and also his attendant temporal freedom."

—**Albert G. Miller**, associate professor emeritus of religion and Africana studies, Oberlin College

"In Christopher Momany's riveting new book, not only are the lives that he describes compelling, but so is his writing. Indeed, Momany draws the reader in, allowing us to identify with the challenges and struggles encountered by five Methodist social activists. Even though they lived nearly two hundred years ago, the ethical dilemmas they faced seem all too familiar. And that's what makes this book critically important for Christians today; these ordinary people acted with courage and conviction. The implication is clear: we, too, can act with similar determination and fearlessness."

—**Douglas Strong**, professor of Wesleyan studies and the history of Christianity, Seattle Pacific University

Compelling Lives

Wesleyan and Methodist Explorations

Compelling Lives

Five Methodist Abolitionists and
the Ideas That Inspired Them

Christopher P. Momany

CASCADE *Books* · Eugene, Oregon

COMPELLING LIVES
Five Methodist Abolitionists and the Ideas That Inspired Them

Wesleyan and Methodist Explorations

Cascade Books
An Imprint of Wipf and Stock Publishers
199 W. 8th Ave., Suite 3
Eugene, OR 97401

www.wipfandstock.com

PAPERBACK ISBN: 978-1-6667-4462-0
HARDCOVER ISBN: 978-1-6667-4463-7
EBOOK ISBN: 978-1-6667-4464-4

Cataloguing-in-Publication data:

Names: Momany, Christopher P., author.

Title: Compelling lives : five Methodist abolitionists and the ideas that inspired them / by Christopher P. Momany.

Description: Eugene, OR: Cascade Books, 2023 | Series: Wesleyan and Methodist Explorations | Includes bibliographical references and index.

Identifiers: ISBN 978-1-6667-4462-0 (paperback) | ISBN 978-1-6667-4463-7 (hardcover) | ISBN 978-1-6667-4464-4 (ebook)

Subjects: LCSH: subject | subject | subject | subject

Classification: CALL NUMBER 2023 (paperback) | CALL NUMBER (ebook)

VERSION NUMBER 07/20/23

For Elizabeth

CONTENTS

ACKNOWLEDGMENTS

I WISH TO EXPRESS gratitude for the people of the First United Methodist Church in Dowagiac, Michigan. Their understanding and support have been inspiring, and their embrace of me as I strive to integrate good scholarship and committed pastoral ministry has tended my soul.

INTRODUCTION

Exactly the Way It Ought to Be

SOJOURNER TRUTH WAS KNOWN for her presence. She possessed a regal bearing, expressed through common identification with others. People who met her knew they were experiencing someone special—at least in part because she brought out the best in them. Presence is a slippery attribute. Unchecked and unrelated to others, it can wander into self-importance. Stereotyped and manipulated by observers, it can be used to control those who wear it. Sojourner Truth was a unique person. She seemed to manage the strengths and vulnerabilities of her identity, and there was a rare genius about her—a genius that was deceptively accessible and, at the same time, unexhausted. Much of her mystique revolved around the fact that she was not constructed; she was real.

According to conventions of her day, Sojourner Truth was not supposed to be so universal. Born into slavery in 1797, along the Dutch-influenced Hudson River Valley and without benefit of formal education, it was easy for those with privilege to write her off. Her self-emancipation as an adult signaled that any underestimation of Truth was a mistake. Yet even Truth's admirers sometimes engaged in patronizing romanticism about her spark, her raw insight and ability to connect with people. Perhaps it is best to name the presence of Sojourner Truth as a form of agency, initiative, even power. At root, she was herself, on her own terms. Period.

Gilbert Haven was different. Lesser known than Sojourner Truth, he was born in 1821 and raised outside of Boston, almost under the shadow of Bunker Hill. The traditions of established patriot ancestry meant much to Haven and his family, and, as a white youth, he enjoyed the privileges of social acceptance and educational opportunity. Gilbert Haven was also perpetual motion—known for his wild red hair and determination to act. Awakened to racial injustice as a youth, he attended Wesleyan University in Connecticut and found himself drawn to the ordained ministry.

Haven worked as a teacher and then the principal of a little academy in Amenia, New York, during the late 1840s. Amenia sits less than fifty miles from the birthplace of Sojourner Truth, though the proximity was more symbolic than connective. Later, when Gilbert Haven served as the pastor of a Methodist church in Northampton, Massachusetts, he became the literal neighbor of Truth. She lived at 35 Park Street in that town for several years. Though from different worlds, with more than twenty years separating them in age, Sojourner Truth and Gilbert Haven became friends.

Both were Methodists, though they embodied different aspects of the tradition. Few today would think of Sojourner Truth as an heir to John Wesley, but from her moment of spiritual awakening that is how she understood herself. Gilbert Haven appeared to plod a more conventional path—raised in the church, educated for ordained ministry—he was even made a bishop following the Civil War. But looks can be deceiving. Haven embraced his spiritual tradition more in terms of theological integrity than institutional membership.

To say that Sojourner Truth and Gilbert Haven were friends is to affirm more than is meant by most invocations of the word "friend." For them, friendship was not a cliché used to paper over unbridgeable difference. It served as an accurate description of their paradoxical relationship—a relationship thrown against the backdrop of our nation's racist expectations and practices. What did such a friendship mean?

Students of Aristotle remind us that many pages in his *Nicomachean Ethics* are devoted to defining true friendship. Friendship, like that other elusive quality—love—is much more difficult to grasp than many assume. Aristotle left an uneven legacy for those committed to social justice, but his understanding of friendship is instructive. Accordingly, he described friendship through a hierarchy of quality and authenticity. Friendship could be built on usefulness, or pleasure, or goodness. The first two are an inferior basis for connection. The last grounds friendship in the value of the other person and in the character that person embodies. Likewise, true friendship can only exist between equals.[1]

The friendship of Sojourner Truth and Gilbert Haven was deeper than some mutual benefit they gave one another and deeper than mere pleasure

1. McKeon, *Introduction to Aristotle*, 509–56.

of acquaintance. They recognized value in each other. Both gained from their association, but that was not why they were friends. Both liked one another and enjoyed the other's personality, but that was not the substance of their rapport. They affirmed a philosophical truth, even if it remained unnamed, that real friends see the unique worth and character of one another. It is a fact that Truth and Haven espoused egalitarian views. They both spoke and lived as if each person on earth shared a common value; all people are equal. But this conviction was not simply theoretical or even writ large. It expressed itself in how they knew each other. In the words of Aristotle, "Friendship is said to be equality."[2]

In 1854 Gilbert Haven preached that overcoming racial injustice required looking at "the heart, at the divine likeness" in people.[3] Table fellowship with friends was especially important to him, and he remarked that Sojourner Truth was "an admirable guest, full of genius and of grace."[4] Haven's commitment to equality was political, but it was also personal. The dynamics of this intriguing friendship reverberated outward when Sojourner Truth visited Gilbert Haven and his family a few years after the Havens moved from Northampton to Wilbraham, Massachusetts. Truth and two friends called on Gilbert and Mary Haven. While sitting at table, enjoying a cup of tea together, the five were interrupted by a man from Haven's congregation. Haven looked up and smiled. The visitor took from his expression a recognition that this shattering of racist conventions, through refreshment and fellowship, modeled the world "exactly the way it ought to be."[5] Such moments of unpretentious community—punctuated by conversation and mutual graciousness—foreshadowed God's coming kingdom.

The five abolitionists featured here were all rooted in something deeper than mere hatred of slavery. They embodied a love for humanity—and not simply humanity in general—but humanity in each person. Their lives unfold throughout this book chronologically, by year of birth. The first chapter provides a wider context and tells a familiar, disappointing tale. The Methodist movement, as inspired by John Wesley, proclaimed that slavery debased the image of God in people. The institutionalization of American Methodism did many things for that movement, but it also provided cover for compromise regarding slavery and for prevailing racist views. Scholars

2. McKeon, *Introduction to Aristotle*, 516.

3. Haven, *National Sermons*, 142.

4. Haven, *National Sermons*, 143.

5. Daniels, *Memorials of Gilbert Haven*, 53.

have charted the decline of American Methodism's witness leading up to the Civil War. It is a shameful legacy.

Yet there were those within the movement who swam against the tide. They might be more difficult to remember because they were not typically movers and shakers at denominational conferences and other official policy-making moments. But that is my point. Those who kept the flame burning—even tending that flame into an unquenchable fire— were seldom granted center stage at established venues. Some, because of their privileged race and gender, were able to rail against injustice within sanctioned gatherings. Most struggled to share their witness outside officialdom. Yet all were self-identified Methodists, and I would argue that bureaucratic power and standard streams of interpretation do not get to decide who counts as a Methodist.

Sojourner Truth (1797–1883) was never considered a Methodist voice among debate at policy-making bodies. Luther Lee (1800–1889) grew up near Truth's Hudson Valley home and then became a Methodist preacher. His privilege gave him access to official arenas, but he made little headway and left to help form the antislavery Wesleyan Methodist Connection. Laura Smith Haviland (1808–98) was born a Quaker and lived in western New York State before moving to Michigan. Many today would be surprised to learn that she identified as a Methodist during the critical years of her antislavery activism and Underground Railroad work. However, Haviland's theological commitments and church membership were thoroughly Wesleyan.

Henry Bibb (1815–54) was born in slavery among the plantations of northern Kentucky. He did not find welcome within any denominational arenas of power, but Bibb was, literally, a card-carrying member of the local Methodist Episcopal Church (as was the man who claimed to own him). Gilbert Haven (1821–80) might seem a typical insider. After all, he became a bishop following the Civil War! But such judgments come too easily. Haven's passion for absolute equality made him more of an outsider than would appear. Even his elevation to the episcopacy led him to a southern location, where he served beyond the dominant chambers of Methodist Episcopal establishment. He was always an alien in a foreign land, despite benefiting from societal privilege.

I say that these five witnesses embodied compelling lives. Their complexity, diversity, and shared values draw us in and hold our attention. They are inspiring and instructive across time, and their most engaging qualities arise from the common ideas that empowered them. Those profound ideas are available to us today.

To Protest as Well as to Acquiesce

The fact that these witnesses for justice stood on the margins or outside the corridors of power leads us to consider their self-understanding. What made them tick? What sustained them and inspired them when the trends of their denominational culture threatened to beat them down? Each of the five people considered here were participants in Methodist bodies. They did not deny the importance of belonging to faith communities. It would not be fair to accuse them of spouting some anti-institutional bias. Those who thrive on being players within organizations often level such charges at critics. The five abolitionists in this study loved Christ's church, but they did not confuse regional bureaucracies with the gospel itself.

Because these abolitionists grasped the difference between human authority (both personal and collective) and divine authority, they relied on spiritual truths, even theological realities, to animate their work. This was not always done in explicit ways, and it was never done as a detached exercise in arcane principles. Their core values, derived from the story of redemption, served as a gyroscopic force which kept them upright when the world was downright lost.

For Sojourner Truth, it was the very law of God written on her heart. For Luther Lee it came through a divine law that cut the clutter of competing loyalties. Laura Haviland found this motivating and stabilizing force in the Bible—claiming that the verities of human rights were spelled out in the sacred text. Henry Bibb discovered his equilibrium in a sense of self created and redeemed by God—a God who gave him voice when the world around him needed honest speech. Gilbert Haven received insight and courage from a unique melding of God's might, a New England heritage, and devotion to human equality. The various motivations behind these prophets may seem unrelated, but each began with reverence for a God who expected something from society and government. Their God did not simply sanction existing social practices. The ordering of community came with divine accountability and was measured by God's law.

Almost one hundred years ago, theologian H. Richard Niebuhr inaugurated his career by writing a well-regarded book, *The Social Sources of Denominationalism* (1929). Niebuhr hoped to trace "the sociological pattern of race, class and sectional interests as it manifested itself in the denominations."[6] This was a groundbreaking study—one that anticipated generations of scholars who sought to understand the way social forces and cultures shape faith traditions and specific faith communities. Yet today it remains an important perspective.

However, in 1937 Niebuhr looked back on his earlier book. He did not retract the salient observations of that text, but he did find the whole analytical framework wanting. Most of all, he concluded that sociological patterns could not exhaust the meaning of spiritual commitment. In short, there was more to faith than mere social forces. His work on *The Kingdom of God in America* acknowledged that collective identities might explain much about the diversity of American religious traditions. Yet this lens could not explain "the faith which is independent, which is aggressive rather than passive, and which molds culture instead of being molded by it."[7] Niebuhr did not deny the importance of sociological dynamics. He simply warned against the kind of reductionism that boils everything about various convictions and practices down to cultural categories.

Some might find this caution a step backward from the insightful analysis of systems. Others might take the warning as license to disregard issues of culture. Both judgments would miss the point. H. Richard Niebuhr did not pine away for less contextual understandings that relied on isolated superheroes of faith. Rather, he pointed out that there are irreducible qualities to communities themselves—and I would add, among the individuals situated within specific communities. Over the centuries, certain theological values nourished a faith that was more than "a mere function of culture."[8] These animating principles fired a desire "to protest as well as to acquiesce, to construct new orders of life as well as to sanctify established orders."[9] These intangibles often created positive change.

The desire to define and understand various cultures is admirable and often associated with a generous approach to social tensions. Grasping the way specific cultures express core values can help us respect the unique vantage point of different communities. However, these definitions and categorizations can also fall into objectification. People might

6. Niebuhr, *Kingdom of God*, ix. I am grateful for the way my friend Douglas M. Strong reminded me of Niebuhr's emphasis.

7. Niebuhr, *Kingdom of God*, x.

8. Niebuhr, *Kingdom of God*, xi.

9. Niebuhr, *Kingdom of God*, xi.

no longer be considered agents of change, despite helpful or oppressive forces. They may instead become little more than expressions of cultural identity, representatives of meticulously numbered traits. At worst, they end up wearing controlling stereotypes. Note how many of today's popular personality inventories and vocational development programs place people in coded categories and even assign them scripted "types." I freely admit that submitting to heavy-handed labels never struck me as an inspiring venture. There is more to being human.

People possess both objective and subjective qualities. They live and move as their own realities and so stand as objective truths. They must be taken seriously, regardless of whether they fit into someone else's explanations or expectations. They also possess a subjectivity—meaning an ability to stand outside of themselves and define their place in the world. This subjectivity does not operate through figments of imagination but from an ability to act within the world as much perhaps as one is acted upon. Reducing everything to social or cultural traits strips people of their sacred subjectivity, their unique genius, their command of at least some prerogative. Individuals do not invent all aspects of reality, and they are often impacted both positively and negatively by larger forces. Moreover, many admirable qualities that nurture strength and prophetic courage are passed down through cultural traditions. Still, inherent dignity means people possess soul and voice and an ability to create meaning.

Henry Bibb was born an enslaved person in Kentucky, struggled, and finally achieved release. When he moved to Canada in 1850, he and others founded a newspaper. It is no accident that this organ was named the *Voice of the Fugitive*. Finding and articulating this voice required struggle, and many were silenced along the road to freedom. But Bibb knew he and others had something to say despite the oppressive systems around them. At the heart of things, Bibb and his colleagues were tired of the dominant culture defining them—especially in ways that were insulting and that served to perpetuate their marginalization. As Afua Cooper has said while speaking of Bibb, those of African descent developed platforms for viewing themselves "in a very self-conscious manner."[10] This heightened awareness demanded that people speak for themselves.

In that same spirit, this book will pay special attention to the words and actions of the major characters, even more so than the later judgments rendered by observers. Meticulous scholarship matters, and more

10. Cooper, "'Doing Battle in Freedom's Cause,'" 299–300.

7

recent attempts to place these lives in a context make sense. Yet a study that underscores the sacred nature of one's initiative, agency, prerogative, and voice must hear what was said by the actors themselves. Secondary evaluations have been consulted and are certainly respected here, but how the protagonists understood their work and their world remains central. There is little more obnoxious than an expert talking over one who is speaking for herself or himself.

There is also a kind of violence in later analysts manipulating and bending the ideas and words of folk who never had a problem speaking up. We may conclude that these witnesses were sometimes mistaken, overbearing, or guilty of their own insensitive assessments, but we should respect the innate value of their voices. They knew what they were doing before we came along.

Anyone who writes this sort of history will inevitably leave fingerprints. There is no way to present the narratives of Sojourner Truth, Luther Lee, Laura Haviland, Henry Bibb, and Gilbert Haven without touching their lives. One can only hope that the contact has not mangled their witness. The goal is to provide an engaging medium for hearing and understanding better what these prophets wished us to hear and understand. Perhaps we might be midwives of the ideas and purposes that were within our antislavery ancestors.

Socrates saw himself as a midwife of the mind—helping others give birth to notions from inside. We flatter ourselves too much if we identify with this iconic figure, but the method is not that different. Some years ago, theologian Nelle Morton described the sacred vocation of "hearing people to speech."[11] This phrase developed from Morton's work with communities of women—women who were tired of being told what to feel or think. Hearing one another through sustained listening offered grace and served as affirmation. It also invited articulation, self-definition, and moments of vital consciousness. The hard work of listening (even to those who died long ago) respects human value, and we are ennobled if we participate in carrying their voices forward.

A Story and a Philosophy to Tell

When I first conceived of writing this book, I knew that I would have to honor established histories of the Methodist relationship with slavery. The

11. See Morton, "Beloved Image: Feminist Imagining."

gold standard study was written by Donald G. Mathews in 1965. His *Slavery and Methodism: A Chapter in American Morality 1780–1845* analyzed institutional shifts that ended in a disappointing witness. Even today one might be pardoned for assuming that a book about American Methodism and slavery would limit itself to this sad trajectory of compromise. Charting the way an admirable stance against slavery devolved into denominational accommodation may seem the obvious approach to our story. Yet such an assumption misses something critical.

For one, this presumption accepts that Methodism per se is identical with institutional organization. The assumption remains strong today. As the Methodist movement in our era experiences conflict and careens toward inevitable division, most conclude that organizational policy is the sole expression of theological tradition. However, some important—even life-giving—truths are lost in this presupposition. The Wesleyan witness is more profound, and many who are nourished by deeper theological emphases might find today's denominational drama, more than anything else, enervating and lacking in imagination.

This is not to deny that we face critical choices of principle in the early twenty-first century. The matters at hand cry for necessary moral discernment. But to say that a denominational culture will either embody or destroy pristine moral clarity is a stretch. Those driven to distraction by official institutional positions and those dreaming of the perfect organization are both overlooking vital theological resources.

Whatever the future brings, it will be but a proximate expression of God's design—a very imperfect expression, at that. Today's struggle is certainly worth pursuing, but it will not create a denominational community that exhausts the gospel itself. After all, you cannot reduce spiritual truths to little more than votes within a legislative body. Our era's competing attempts to make official machinery support this or that perspective mirror the intrigues of American Methodism during the 1830s and 1840s. It is a mistake to assume that the policies of a formal conference sum up the entirety of Wesleyan meaning in our century. It is also a mistake to conclude that we can understand all there is to understand about Methodism's debate over slavery by documenting nineteenth-century legislation among official gatherings.

In some practical, even colloquial, sense we must be open to the philosophical sensitivities of abolitionists. This does not mean that we should take formal philosophical theories and force them into the conversation. It does mean that we must get at the motivating patterns of thought embraced by antislavery activists. Some of these ideals were more like embedded principles that came alive in the heat of advocacy. Others were acknowledged frameworks of conviction invoked by those who acted for justice. The world of ideas does not fit neatly into heavy-handed readings of the movement, and it would be easy to dismiss these patterns of the mind. Yet treating animating principles as inadmissible evidence distorts the record. Such disregard is also a clumsy wielding of interpretive power.

Power is not necessarily a bad thing and can be harnessed to advance equitable emphases. However, those who ignore a deeper look at abolitionist principles and the ways they were expressed through individual lives engage in dehumanizing behavior, and this is the sort of thing that advocates for justice find, understandably, offensive. The funny thing about power is the way it is almost universally seen as bad when expressed by someone else but redeeming when it suits my agenda. This dynamic presents an equal opportunity danger. It is not only a weakness of those defending the status quo. It is also a double-edged sword for those who seek to make systems more just. We must tread lightly when seeking to understand the Methodist witness against slavery. Above all, we must listen to the prophets.

Years ago, writer Carl Sandburg told of a Civil War soldier who stumbled onto a dead comrade in the wilderness of Chancellorsville, Virginia. I lived for a time in those same woods as an undergraduate intern and battlefield interpreter for the National Park Service. It is a dense place— with weather-beaten trench systems, thick brambles, decomposing leaves, flashes of sunlight cutting through a crowded canopy of trees. During the Civil War, this dead soldier had been forgotten and then discovered months later, sitting with his back against a tree, "looking at first sight almost alive enough to hold a conversation with the living."[12] Sandburg added, "He seemed to have a story and a philosophy to tell if the correct approach were made and he could be led into a quiet discussion."[13]

The man who stumbled upon this ghostly figure was frightened and painfully aware that he had "interrupted a silence where the slants of silver moons and the music of varying rains kept company with the one against the tree who sat so speechless, though having much to say."[14] A story and philosophy to tell. Few would doubt the story, but philosophy is a different

12. Sandburg, *Abraham Lincoln*, 105.
13. Sandburg, *Abraham Lincoln*, 105.
14. Sandburg, *Abraham Lincoln*, 105.

matter. Philosophy sounds so formal, structured, cold—almost too cold, even for one reposing in death. But what if philosophy is as much animating purpose and commitment as it is articulated principle? Anyone struggling to make sense of things like freedom and slavery would embody some such philosophy, and we would be better for hearing it. What if our artful listening could hear across time, especially those who struggled to live for human dignity? Is it pure imagination to hope we might hear such witnesses to speech? Listening is a grace that may evoke eloquence.

Chapter I

A TALE OF TWO LEGACIES

Athanasius against the World

THE MURDER OF GEORGE Floyd during the summer of 2020 changed things. To say this is no stroke of insight. Of course, such a tragedy should elicit change. Yet this imperative cannot be taken for granted. Similar brutality has often gone unaddressed, and little has changed. Not this time. The death of Floyd ignited a season of open unrest and predictable denial. It also forced millions of Christians to examine themselves. Some summoned familiar arguments on behalf of racial justice. Others clung to defenses of law and order.

The impulses of Americans revealed competing ideologies—incompatible theories regarding human nature and destiny. Many embracing the language of "evangelical" Christianity threw their weight behind secular abuses of power. Those desiring to create a better society tended to avoid all identification with traditional beliefs.

Among this cacophony of voices appeared an outlier—a different angle of vision. Writing for *The Washington Post*, Michael Gerson offered a column with the unlikely title "What One of the Founders of Evangelicalism Can Teach Us about Racism."[1] This piece invoked both John Wesley's unyielding opposition to slavery and his evangelical faith. In short, Gerson refused to accept the assumption that evangelical tradition has always backed the misuse of power. Moreover, this argument was not a defense of conservative Christianity. It spoke as a judgment upon the movement and a call to embrace the prophetic past.

1. Gerson, "What One of the Founders."

John Wesley (1703–91) can be counted a genuine parent of the evangelical movement. His vocation as an Anglican clergyperson with a heart for renewal made him so. Wesley expressed a faith that stressed salvation by grace through faith for a lost world. Equally clear was his stance against social injustice. Still, admiring an eighteenth-century figure does not require one to overlook flaws within that person's life or to assume that such a witness bears a prescription for all of today's problems. Then there is Michael Gerson—a complicated contemporary observer in his own right. Gerson's record as a neo-conservative will put many off. But perhaps this juxtaposition of identities and emphases makes a point. The secular left does not own all passion for authentic justice. The racist right must not determine who counts as a follower of Christ. God's authority surpasses these frameworks.

Gerson asserts that "according to modern political categories, Wesley would be an unlikely recruit to social justice agitation. But the founder of Methodism became one of the first major public figures in Britain to call for the abolition of slavery for a particular reason: The evangelical conception of salvation dictated a high view of human worth."[2] Accordingly, this worth is created by God and is not subject to the manipulation of social forces. Also, in Wesley's particular brand of theology, the salvation offered by Jesus was not reserved for some nominally elect people. Grace came to each and all. The egalitarian implications of this approach were astounding.

Many aspects of John Wesley's life are disputed: his precise standing between the Catholic and Reformed traditions or the exact impact of his concern for the poor. The fact that he managed a stout witness against slavery does not mean he was free from racial bias or completely beyond the damaging prejudices of his era. Scholarship has made us aware of his faults in this regard.[3] His clearest witness against slavery is found in the 1774 tract, "Thoughts upon Slavery."

This twenty-one-page document, written the year before the American Revolution, remains remarkable for several reasons. First, the content of the missive pulls no punches. It condemns slavery without qualification, and it does not buy self-justifying arguments from oppressors. Enslaved people were typically cast as dangerous, and the privileged weaponized a fear of uprising. To this Wesley responded, "What wonder, if they should cut your throat? And if they did, whom could you thank for it but yourself?"[4] The establishment victimized innocent Africans and then portrayed them as

2. Gerson, "What One of the Founders."
3. Field, "Imaging the 'Exotic Other,'" 64–75.
4. Wesley, "Thoughts upon Slavery," 75.

threats to society. Wesley would not have it. His sympathy and empathy were clearly on the side of those whose very lives had been stolen.

More subtly, a deep reading of the tract reveals that the way it was argued equaled the impact of its content. Wesley made his point through a very meticulous method. For one so irrevocably committed to the evangelical narrative of creation, fall, and redemption, John Wesley employed particularly philosophical principles to state his case. Popular appraisal likes to remember the way Wesley claimed to be "a man of one book"— the Bible.[5] However the "Thoughts upon Slavery" sought to undermine cruelty without specific reliance on the sacred text. Wesley endeavored to demonstrate slavery's injustice, even while "setting the Bible out of the question."[6] Certainly, the founder of Methodism considered the Bible to be an essential window on truth, but he also appreciated the way specifically philosophical ideas could carry his argument.

Today it is not considered fashionable to highlight these aspects of Wesley's writing. For several decades scholars have labored under an intellectual obligation to badmouth the Enlightenment era (approximately 1650–1800) and its philosophical notions. Yet if someone as devoted to the Bible as John Wesley could blend the best principles of his age into an attack on slavery, we ought to reconsider our assumptions. This is not to say that Wesley only parroted the words of Enlightenment thinkers, but his campaign against slavery did draw from specific sources.

The "Thoughts upon Slavery" is constructed in five sections. Each part weaves the ideas and language of other advocates through Wesley's own argument. The person who perhaps influenced Wesley the most was Quaker abolitionist Anthony Benezet (1713–84). Benezet emerged from a French Huguenot family that fled their homeland amid persecution. They joined the Religious Society of Friends in England and later moved to America, settling in Philadelphia. Anthony Benezet's tracts blasting slavery spoke to John Wesley. As much as 30 percent of Wesley's "Thoughts upon Slavery" is drawn from Benezet's book *Some Historical Account of Guinea* (1771).[7]

However, the opening section of Wesley's piece is indebted to a different source—the thought of Granville Sharp. Sharp (1735–1813) was an English biblical scholar, commentator, and literary savant who took up the cause of abolition. Born in Durham, he transformed a rather ordinary

5. Wesley, *Works of John Wesley*, 105.
6. Wesley, "Thoughts upon Slavery," 70.
7. Baker, "Origins, Character, and Influence," 79.

education into a rigorous journey of self-development. Sharp taught himself Greek and eventually mastered Hebrew—all to probe the world of ideas and argument. In 1765 Sharp met Jonathan Strong, an enslaved man from Barbados. Strong had been assaulted by the person claiming to own him, and Granville Sharp provided financial support for medical care as well as legal advocacy. Through it all, Sharp turned his intense self-motivation toward study of the English law. Eventually Strong was granted freedom, but the astounding brutality of his treatment and the lethargic legal process disgusted Granville Sharp. The first section of John Wesley's "Thoughts" builds upon the framework of Sharp's writing.[8]

The second section of "Thoughts" provides a context for considering and condemning slavery. Here Wesley addresses the regions of Africa from which enslaved people were taken. He also speaks to the cultural identities and strengths of those captured. Wesley offers his own introductory material to this section but relies heavily on Anthony Benezet's *Guinea*. In fact, the major portion of Wesley's tract here is a paraphrase from Benezet.[9]

Section three of "Thoughts" is more eclectic but owes most of its argument to a combination of Benezet and Granville Sharp. In this movement of the tract, Wesley emphasizes the heinous nature of abduction, transatlantic journey, and treatment in America.[10]

By the time Wesley opens a fourth section, the reader is prepared to consider a forceful blending of philosophical principles. Borrowing from legendary jurist William Blackstone, Wesley judged slavery a violation of natural rights.

John Wesley remains known for his "conservative" attitudes about government and society, but this did not necessarily mean what many today think it means. He was certainly, in most respects, a Tory, and yet he defined a Tory as one who held "God, not the people, to be the origin of all civil power."[11] Viewed from the perch of American revolutionary thought, this may seem to overlook the consent of the people. Yet the perspective featured a transcendent standard of justice. This emphasis upon God's prerogative was not an attempt to protect the arbitrary desires of king and

---

8. Wiecek, *Sources of Antislavery Constitutionalism*, 25–26. See also: Smith, *John Wesley and Slavery*, 76–77.

9. Baker, "Origins, Character, and Influence," 79.

10. Baker, "Origins, Character, and Influence," 80.

11. Wesley, "Letter to the Gentleman's Magazine," 360.

gentry. When Wesley spoke of divine authority, he meant just that—a righteousness beyond human power and manipulation.

Wesley's conviction emerged loud and clear as he addressed the supposed legality of slavery. To those who asserted that various codes upholding slavery were legal, Wesley shot back: "The grand plea is, 'They are authorized by law.' But can law, human law, change the nature of things? Can it turn darkness into light, or evil into good? By no means. Notwithstanding ten thousand laws, right is right, and wrong is wrong still."[12] This thoughtfully assembled argument served as spadework for later Methodist abolitionists who preached a "higher law."

The higher law argument against slavery took many forms over the next century. Some created an impulsive anti-institutionalism that bordered on anarchism. This was not Wesley's approach. His invocation of divine authority was more substantial, more deliberate, more reflective. He knew that raw anti-establishment resistance did little to offer a better way. The divine law had to be grounded in something deeper.

Therefore, Wesley linked God's law with an understanding of how the world and its people are intended to live. There was a harmonious design to human nature and destiny. When it came to matters of justice, Wesley emphasized natural rights. His higher law was best reflected by relationships that respected such rights. After stating that people captured from Africa have the same natural rights as those born in England, Wesley thundered, "I absolutely deny all slave-holding to be consistent with any degree of natural justice."[13] He drew a stark contrast between the way the world was supposed to function and the brutal way it was being managed by those who perpetuated slavery.

Americans are often reminded of the way John Wesley opposed the American Revolution—as if this fact somehow made him less committed to Enlightenment convictions around human rights. Yet his understandings of right and wrong—justice and oppression—were uncompromising, and he was not afraid to speak from the principles of his age. We do ourselves and John Wesley a disservice when we overlook his reliance upon eighteenth-century ideas.

The fifth and final section of "Thoughts upon Slavery" seeks to apply points underscored in earlier movements. Wesley's type of application was really a bare-knuckle indictment of those who benefited from slavery. He

12. Wesley, "Thoughts upon Slavery," 70.
13. Wesley, "Thoughts upon Slavery," 70.

calls out a wide range of abusers and condemns their behavior before ending on a more philosophical note. Near the close of his tract, he writes, "Liberty is the right of every human creature, as soon as he breathes the vital air; and no human law can deprive him of that right which he derives from the law of nature."[14] This appeal to the law of nature lived beyond Wesley's day and found its way into nineteenth-century abolitionist publications.[15]

Writing near the end of the twentieth century, Leon Hynson argued that Wesley's "Thoughts upon Slavery" was, in fact, "a declaration of human rights."[16] Hynson's language is reminiscent of the *Universal Declaration of Human Rights*, the post-World War II framework approved by the United Nations in 1948.[17] Recent decades have seen the whole human rights perspective come under fire for reflecting rather limited, European ideas of justice. The criticism deserves serious attention. Yet Hynson did not argue that John Wesley prefigured every twentieth-century emphasis regarding rights. He simply suggested that Wesley's "Thoughts" benefited from certain Enlightenment-era ideals.

For instance, Hynson wrote that Wesley's tract "deliberately appeals to normal eighteenth-century rationale such as the natural rights of justice, life, liberty, and happiness."[18] Perhaps most insightful is the comparison between those parts in "Thoughts" that rely on Anthony Benezet and those that are the unique creation of Wesley's mind and pen. Hynson noted, "In the last third of Wesley's tract he departs from Benezet's affective and sympathetic arguments and begins to marshall his own highly logical, legal and natural right arguments."[19] Some will conclude that Hynson overstated his case, but many can appreciate the way Wesley departed from entirely biblical language to embrace the better principles of his age.

Today's world of theological scholarship resists celebrating much of anything related to the Enlightenment, but then again, scholars are as embedded in the trends of their times as anyone else. It is notoriously difficult to view one's own perspective through an independent lens. To appreciate John Wesley's use of Enlightenment ideas is not to deny problems

14. Wesley, "Thoughts upon Slavery," 79.

15. See especially Matlack, *Life of Rev. Orange Scott*, 142.

16. Hynson, "Wesley's 'Thoughts upon Slavery.'"

17. Roosevelt et al., *Universal Declaration of Human Rights*.

18. Hynson, "Wesley's 'Thoughts upon Slavery,'" 46.

19. Hynson, "Wesley's 'Thoughts upon Slavery,'" 46.

with his approach. However, ignoring this side of Wesley says much more about our age than his.

By the end of his life, Wesley made clear that he saw a conflict between the world God intended and the world as corrupted by humanity. This did not mean that everything around him required judgment and holy resistance, but it did suggest that his war against slavery was just that—a battle against prevailing values. Wesley's last letter, written to William Wilberforce (the English abolitionist) in 1791, makes this point. He underscored God's appointment of Wilberforce as *"Athanasius contra mundum"* (Athanasius against the world).[20] This phrase, recalling the early church leader who stood against error in his day, reflected Wesley's essential vision. He saw himself not as a renegade sowing unprecedented notions but as an advocate for divine authority, deploying the best ideas of his era.

Repugnant to Reason and the Principles of Natural Law

An underrated aspect of John Wesley's indictment against slavery can be traced to the iconic English jurist William Blackstone (1723–80). The pivotal fourth section of "Thoughts upon Slavery" owes much to the thinking and writing of this legendary judge, a man described by Wesley as "that great ornament of his profession."[21]

William Blackstone was born on July 10, 1723, in Cheapside, London. Following the death of his parents, an uncle, surgeon Thomas Bigg, supported young William and his brothers. With the advocacy of this benevolent relative, Blackstone received an education at the Charterhouse, London, and then moved on to Oxford. By 1740 young William began studies in the law and added wide reading of other subjects. He turned his attention to the common law in 1746.[22]

At All Souls College, Oxford, Blackstone began a tenure of administrative and academic work that led him to a momentous decision in 1753. That summer he decided to offer a private, independent course of lectures to supplement the formal curriculum of the university. This was not an entirely new way of teaching, but it became the initiative that made a name for William Blackstone. Until that time, the English law was a complicated

20. Wesley, "Letter to a Friend," 153.

21. Wesley, "Thoughts upon Slavery," 70.

22. Prest, "Blackstone," 6:10–11.

web of precedent and practice developed outside the classical training of university education. Blackstone brought the day-to-day traditions of his nation inside the university, gave them a structured interpretation, and laid the groundwork for later legal theory.[23]

Before Blackstone's lectures (and later publication of them) the term "civil law" was reserved for the study of Roman law and its ancient principles. Today one might dismiss William Blackstone as some dour eighteenth-century elitist who perpetuated the stifling machinery of English law, but in his day, Blackstone was a maverick—intent on bringing the living, working pursuit of justice inside university education. By 1758 he was appointed the first Vinerian professor of the English Common Law at Oxford (named after Charles Viner), and the English traditions of law were established as their own formal discipline.[24]

The first volume of Blackstone's lectures was published in 1765 under the title *Commentaries on the Laws of England*. More than two centuries of reading and interpretation have focused on the second section of the introduction. Here Blackstone made clear that he considered humanity subject to the authority of a holy God. People are entirely dependent beings and properly accountable to a transcendent standard. What is more, this standard was identified with God's will. The Oxford professor explained, "This will of his maker is called the law of nature," and the law of nature was known by reason.[25]

A few paragraphs after this discussion Blackstone made a statement that shaped generations of legal theory. He contended that the law of nature, "being co-eval with mankind and dictated by God himself, is of course superior in obligation to any other. It is binding over all the globe, in all countries, and at all times: no human laws are of any validity, if contrary to this; and such of them as are valid derive all their force, and all their authority, mediately or immediately, from this original."[26] In short, all authentic human laws received their standing from resemblance to the original. At best, they were transcripts of nature's law.

Blackstone conceded that reason is an imperfect aid in grasping the natural law, and so he reserved a place for immediate and direct revelation. This he termed the "revealed or divine law," and he held that such

---

23. Prest, "Blackstone," 6:11–12.
24. Prest, "Blackstone," 6:12–13.
25. Blackstone, *Commentaries on the Laws of England: A Facsimile*, 39.
26. Blackstone, *Commentaries on the Laws of England: A Facsimile*, 41.

truths were found in the Scriptures.[27] Later abolitionists would appeal to something very much like Blackstone's law of nature, and sometimes they would call it a "divine law," regardless of whether it came from the Bible. The overwhelming takeaway for students of the *Commentaries* was this contrast between godly and human authority and the measurement of all earthly law by a transcendent standard.

Since the late nineteenth century, Blackstone's conception of the law of nature (or natural law) has fallen out of favor. Sophisticated developments, typically driven by secular assumptions, considered the Oxford commentator a sluggish purveyor of traditional religious ideas. Blackstone was relegated to the musty basements of law libraries, remembered only as a dull cataloger of the human condition. He was dismissed as unequal to the newer legal questions arising from complex social forces. By the opening of the twentieth century leading intellectuals questioned any appeal to eternal standards. The new perspectives saw human legislation as determining its own validity. There was no higher law, according to this view.

Yet the world and thinking of William Blackstone informed much of John Wesley's objection to slavery. The fourth section of Wesley's "Thoughts" reflected a strict adherence to universal standards, and the founder of Methodism included a lengthy quote taken directly from the *Commentaries*. Blackstone critiqued "the right of slavery," as understood by Roman jurist Justinian.[28] Given that the English law articulated in the *Commentaries* was posed in contrast with Roman law, we should not be surprised to hear Blackstone conclude, "The three origins of the right of slavery assigned by Justinian, are all of them built upon false foundations."[29] John Wesley repeated this argument and borrowed Blackstone's natural law emphasis.[30]

Many late-eighteenth century and early-nineteenth century abolitionists looked to the English law in general, and to Blackstone in particular, when arguing that slavery violated a higher law. After all, the same paragraph used by Blackstone to refute Justinian contained a categorial declaration: Slavery was judged "repugnant to reason, and the principles of natural law."[31] The matter appeared to be settled.

27. Blackstone, *Commentaries on the Laws of England: A Facsimile*, 42.

28. Blackstone, *Commentaries on the Laws of England: A Facsimile*, 411.

29. Blackstone, *Commentaries on the Laws of England: A Facsimile*, 411.

30. Wesley, "Thoughts upon Slavery," 70–71.

31. Blackstone, *Commentaries on the Laws of England: A Facsimile*, 411.

One who worked from this framework was Granville Sharp, the man who influenced Wesley, along with Anthony Benezet. Sharp embraced the cause of the enslaved man, Jonathan Strong, just as the *Commentaries on the Laws of England* rolled off the press. By 1769 he published his own tome with the unwieldy title *A Representation of the Injustice and Dangerous Tendency of Tolerating Slavery in England.* Sharp insisted that "true justice makes no respect of persons, and can never deny to any one that blessing to which all mankind have an undoubted right, their *natural liberty*."[32] This work shaped much of John Wesley's thinking on the subject, and it complemented the legal theory of William Blackstone.

Yet the relationship between theory and action is never as seamless as many would like. Between 1765 and 1768, William Blackstone revised his condemnation of slavery. The first edition of the *Commentaries* suggested that proper English law allowed for no toleration of human bondage. The third edition, published in 1768, backpedaled. In 1765 Blackstone had stated that an enslaved person brought to England immediately "falls under the protection of the laws, and with regard to all natural rights becomes . . . a freeman."[33] By 1768 he qualified this language and added that even following such freedom, "the master's right to his service may probably still continue."[34] The ambiguity caused by Blackstone's revision was not helpful to advocates like Granville Sharp.

Sharp clung to the first statement that English law necessitated unqualified freedom. He also sought out a specific case that would substantiate this principle. By the early 1770s Sharp found his opportunity. An enslaved man, James Somerset, had been brought to England from Virginia and was subsequently threatened with sale to Jamaica. Somerset escaped but was recaptured. Charles Sewart, the person claiming to own Somerset, was challenged by antislavery advocates who wished to make a statement for liberty. The case of *Somerset v. Stewart* changed all subsequent conversations about slavery and the laws of England. In 1772 Chief Justice of the King's Bench William Murray (Lord Mansfield) ruled against Stewart and recognized Somerset's freedom. Mansfield insisted that his decision was limited to the case at hand, but the implications of his judgment took on a life of their own.

32. Sharp, *Representation of the Injustice*, 38.
33. Blackstone, *Commentaries on the Laws of England: A Facsimile*, 123.
34. Blackstone, *Commentaries on the Laws of England, Book the First*, 127.

Part of Lord Mansfield's reasoning relied on a distinction between natural and "positive" law. Responding to the claims of Charles Stewart, Mansfield ruled, "The state of slavery is of such a nature, that it is incapable of being introduced on any reasons, moral or political, but only by positive law. . . . It is so odious, that nothing can be suffered to support it, but positive law. Whatever inconveniences, therefore, may follow from the decision, I cannot say this case is allowed or approved by the law of England."[35] James Somerset was released.

Technically speaking, Mansfield did not say that positive law was powerless against natural law, but by driving such a wedge between the two, he opened the door for more aggressive abolitionist arguments. Antislavery legal theorists took note, and several sought to extend the meaning of Mansfield's finding. It became part of the antislavery canon to hold that positive law was always and everywhere secondary to natural law, while also holding that natural law was completely opposed to slavery.

Therefore, the combination of William Blackstone's moderately antislavery teaching and Lord Mansfield's limited ruling lived beyond the intentions of their authors. Later editions of the *Commentaries* struggled to clarify the qualification that people may remain obligated to service in England, even after falling under legal protection. For instance, Blackstone's statement that masters "may probably" retain a right to service was changed in a prominent American edition of 1807. This American printing read that the right to demand service "may *possibly*" continue.[36] We might find this to be a lot of noxious hairsplitting, but it demonstrated the way later editors and commentators struggled to find consistency in Blackstone.

One thing was certain, advocates for all kinds of freedoms conscripted the language and logic of William Blackstone to make their case. Even the patriot cause in America included creative appeals to Blackstone. Notably, young Alexander Hamilton's defense of the Continental Congress demanded that his opponent apply himself "without delay, to the study of the law of nature."[37] Hamilton continued that the deity has "constituted an eternal and immutable law, which is . . . obligatory upon all mankind, prior to any human institution whatever."[38] It should not come as a surprise that the young patriot grounded this claim in what was probably the

---

35. Somerset v. Stewart, *Howell's State Trials*, 82.

36. Blackstone, *Commentaries on the Laws of England, In Four Books*, 127.

37. Hamilton, *Farmer Refuted*, 5.

38. Hamilton, *Farmer Refuted*, 6.

most quoted passage of William Blackstone: the description of nature's law, which is superior to all earthly enactments.

For the record, William Blackstone never intended to inspire revolution in America, and he would have no doubt found Hamilton's argument a misappropriation of his legal philosophy. However, there is a fine line between the misapplication of principle and following it to its logical conclusion. Just as many abolitionists stretched Lord Mansfield's decision, advocates for political freedom sometimes invoked Blackstone's tenets.

The complexity of Anglo-American relations in the 1770s led to situations where staunch antislavery activists were firmly against the American Revolution. It also led to situations where ardent revolutionaries were silent or complicit regarding slavery. For many in England, American grievances reeked of hypocrisy. This was John Wesley's view. When revolutionaries in America claimed to be enslaved by the British government, Wesley called them out. How could they whine about their treatment when so many Americans held African people in literal bondage? Much colonial revolutionary rhetoric did not pass the smell test.[39]

For his part, Granville Sharp combined a lifelong opposition to slavery with support for the American cause. Sharp had concluded that the colonists in America were "pleading their natural and legal rights."[40] At the beginning of the conflict, Sharp was a British armaments clerk, and his conscience would not let him rest. He first took a leave of absence from his post and eventually resigned in protest.[41]

Following the American Revolution, various forms of the natural law or higher law argument were employed by abolitionists. Some of these frameworks emphasized natural rights apart from explicitly theological backing, but others were almost conflated with biblical principles. In America, the higher law perspective became identified with New England antislavery activism, and yet the doctrine found expression in many regions of the young republic and across many religious traditions. Scholars often assumed that the antislavery movement depended upon belief in a higher law, but the conviction was never really explored in depth. Finally, in 1960, Louis Filler's classic study *The Crusade Against Slavery* called for more rigorous examination.[42] Ten years later George Carter accepted the challenge and wrote a PhD

39. Wesley, "Calm Address," 81.

40. Hoare, *Memoirs of Granville Sharp*, 122.

41. Hoare, *Memoirs of Granville Sharp*, 123–26.

42. Filler, *Crusade against Slavery*, 98.

dissertation on "The Use of the Doctrine of Higher Law in the American Anti-Slavery Crusade, 1830–1860."[43]

American Methodists from the time of Revolution to the Civil War also invoked the higher law, often in oblique and almost unconscious ways. Yet like John Wesley, they were convinced that right was right and wrong was wrong. The clash of divine and worldly values demanded that they take a stand.

Every Principle of the Revolution

America during the Revolution (1775–83) was not particularly supportive of the Methodist movement. John Wesley's Tory perspective and Methodism's direct linkage to the parent country worked against growth in America. Well-worn histories recall that most of Wesley's appointed missionaries either returned to England or went to Canada. The American-born preachers (along with Francis Asbury) kept Methodism's flame lit, and by the end of the Revolution, the movement was headed for an independence not unlike the republic.[44]

The Methodist conference in America addressed slavery, even before the creation of an independent church. Minutes from 1780 included the statement that "slavery is contrary to the laws of God, man, and nature, and hurtful to society; contrary to the dictates of conscience and true religion; and doing what we would not others should do unto us."[45] The combination of concepts, themes, and principles in this declaration is instructive. Something akin to the natural law or the law of nature grounded the conference's witness, along with an appeal to conscience. We should also note the way the Golden Rule was cited. There were, of course, several biblical reasons for opposing slavery, but the reference to some overarching law demonstrated that Wesley's argument from 1774 took root in America.

The watershed year for American Methodists came in 1784, as the celebrated Christmas Conference established the Methodist Episcopal Church. Conference minutes declared that slavery is "contrary to the Golden Law of God on which hang all the Law and the Prophets, and the unalienable Rights of Mankind, as well as every Principle of the Revolution."[46] Perhaps

43. Carter, "Use of the Doctrine of Higher Law."
44. Norwood, *Story of American Methodism*, 84–88.
45. Quoted in Birney, *American Churches*, 10.
46. Coke and Asbury, *Minutes of Several Conversations*, 15.

most striking is the reference to "every Principle of the Revolution." One year after the formal recognition of the United States by Britain, American Methodists borrowed ideas from the Revolution to oppose slavery. For a movement that was suspect during times of war, this association with revolutionary ideas made a statement. Not only was the Methodist Episcopal body a uniquely American church, it was also a church that understood the national creed in antislavery terms.

Among those in attendance at the Christmas Conference was Harry Hosier (1750?–1806). As an African American, he faced much opposition but demonstrated profound gifts for leadership. He traveled with bishops Francis Asbury and Thomas Coke and developed a reputation as one of the best preachers in the land. But he was not accorded a vote at the Christmas Conference, and this injustice must be remembered. Still, Hosier was there, and that meant something.[47]

Harry Hosier (1750?–1806) traveled with early Methodist bishops Francis Asbury and Thomas Coke and was known for his powerful preaching.

Image Courtesy of The General Commission on Archives and History, The United Methodist Church

47. Norwood, *The Story of American Methodism*, 168.

Not all Americans or even most of them read the nation's founding principles as a call to end slavery, but a significant part of American Methodism did. One blazing example of this perspective came in the form of Ezekiel Cooper.

Ezekiel Cooper (1763–1847) was born in Caroline County, Maryland, and raised as a nominal member of the Church of England. Around his thirteenth year he encountered Methodist preachers. The iconic Freeborn Garrettson even visited the Cooper home and made a lasting impression. Young Ezekiel wrestled mightily to know God. One day he found himself walking in the woods and began to pray. Cooper experienced "the infinite fullness of Christ" and the embrace of his maker.[48] He joined a Methodist community and was supported through the trials of discipleship. Finally, in 1784 he determined to be a preacher.

Notably, Cooper began his formal ministry as the Methodist Episcopal Church was born. He served on Long Island and in New Jersey, Baltimore, and Annapolis, Maryland. It was from Annapolis that he engaged in public debate over slavery. On July 4, 1790, Cooper delivered a sermon within sight of the Maryland State House, and his discourse blasted American hypocrisy regarding slavery.[49] This was followed by a series of letters in various publications.

On November 8, 1790, writing for the *Maryland Gazette*, Cooper asserted that freedom "is by the law of nature granted to every man, the 'just due of every man.'"[50] Therefore "any law is inhuman and unjust that counteracts the law of God in nature."[51] He continued to advance an argument reminiscent of William Blackstone in April of 1791: "All truly human laws agree with the law of nature in every thing consistent with society."[52] This last post, penned from Alexandria, Virginia, also addressed a particularly disturbing trend among proslavery apologists: the use of Scripture to defend human bondage.

48. Phoebus, *Beams of Light*, 18.
49. Phoebus, *Beams of Light*, 106–7.
50. Phoebus, *Beams of Light*, 316.
51. Phoebus, *Beams of Light*, 317.
52. Phoebus, *Beams of Light*, 325.

Ezekiel Cooper (1763–1847) preached that slavery was entirely
inconsistent with America's founding principles.

Image Courtesy of The General Commission on Archives and History,
The United Methodist Church

As the nineteenth century opened, some Methodists charged that abolitionists drank too deeply from the Enlightenment well of human rights. To oppose these notions, many claimed that proper biblical exposition supported slavery. The debate was never this simple, of course, and there were those who made profound antislavery arguments from Scripture. But the die was cast.

By 1836, southern Methodists were more than eager to accuse abolitionists of undermining biblical authority. This was especially the case in South Carolina. The annual conference there condemned antislavery agitation and charged, "We consider and believe that the Holy Scriptures, so far from giving any countenance to this delusion, do unequivocally authorise the relation of master and slave."[53] Moreover, the rationale for this assertion spoke volumes. The same annual conference attributed abolitionist views to "a false philosophy, overreaching or setting aside the scriptures through a vain conceit of a higher moral refinement."[54] A suspicion of certain Enlightenment ideas was never far behind the biblical defense of slavery.

Perhaps the best-known proslavery biblical interpreter to arise from South Carolina was William Capers. Capers (1790–1855) grew up near Charleston and studied law in his early adulthood. Before long he experienced a call to preach and, in the words of Donald Mathews, "rejected Blackstone for the Bible."[55] This meant only that Capers shifted from law to ministry, but the language could not be more apt. Young William left philosophical conceptions of right and wrong behind and employed the Scriptures to defend slavery.

Responding to abolitionists from the Boston publication *Zion's Herald*, Capers claimed that he considered "the Scriptures to be the rule, and the only rule, for determining what is, and what is not, moral evil. . . . Slavery, *simply as such* . . . is not a moral evil."[56] This argument appeared in many forms throughout the 1830s.

Finally, the General Conference of the Methodist Episcopal Church, meeting at Cincinnati in 1836, signaled that crisis was coming. Abolitionists, organized by Orange Scott (1800–1847), sought to debate slavery, but the conference body issued a strong rebuke. There would be no open and honest engagement. As Donald Mathews put it, the General Conference decided that "the only scriptural way to deal with slavery was to refrain from discussing it."[57] While many asserted that bondage found support in the Bible, others avoided the question altogether—arguing that whatever its moral standing, slavery was a matter of civil law and not church policy.

As for direct appeals to the Bible in defense of slavery, the crowning audacity came when Bishop Elijah Hedding (1780–1852) presided over annual conference sessions during the fall of 1837. The bishop suggested that it was not slavery itself which deserved condemnation but the mistreatment of enslaved people. Appropriate slavery might exist where enslaved persons

53. *Minutes of the South Carolina Conference*, 20.

54. *Minutes of the South Carolina Conference*, 20.

55. Mathews, *Slavery and Methodism*, 69.

56. Capers, *Southern Christian Advocate*, 150.

57. Mathews, *Slavery and Methodism*, 144.

were treated as one would want to be treated under similar conditions. This amounted to an exoneration of slavery by invoking the Golden Rule.[58] Luther Lee (1800–1889), who would soon leave the Methodist Episcopal Church over the matter, participated in one of these conferences. Lee later recalled that the bishop had said, "The right to hold a slave is founded upon this rule, 'All things whatsoever ye would that men should do to you, do you even so to them; for this is the law and the prophets.'"[59] Hedding evidently did not grasp the irony (let alone hypocrisy) of distorting a biblical principle that had been cited by Methodists in 1780 to condemn slavery!

Traditional readings of Methodist history have focused on the fateful General Conference of 1844 and the breakup of the denomination over slavery, but the underlying conflict of values has received less attention. The fracture of 1844 must be read as one moment in a long narrative of moral concessions, and the years following schism added their own chapters to the story.

The Methodist Episcopal Church was already in pieces when the United States Congress passed the so-called Compromise of 1850. This legislation strengthened the Fugitive Slave Act of 1793, making every American legally responsible for returning self-emancipated people to bondage, and there were severe penalties for those who aided seekers of freedom. The Methodist attempt to treat civil law and church law as two distinct and yet compatible authorities fell apart. Civil law claimed superiority and demanded that everyone in the nation uphold the institution of slavery.

Into this whirlwind stepped Senator William H. Seward of New York, who argued against the Compromise and added that there was a "higher law" than the Constitution which rightfully claimed the loyalty of Americans.[60] Seward was immediately attacked by Southern interests for challenging the supremacy of civil law (which happened to be protecting slavery just then). However, some Methodists, drawing on Wesley's transcendent distinction between right and wrong, came to Seward's defense. William Hosmer (1810–89) was one such Methodist.

Hosmer hailed from Massachusetts and lived for much of his life in Auburn, New York. Auburn was also home to William H. Seward—and, later, Harriet Tubman. Between 1848 and 1856, Hosmer served as the editor of the *Northern Christian Advocate*, a publication sponsored by the

58. Mathews, *Slavery and Methodism*, 155–56.
59. Lee, *Autobiography*, 136.
60. Seward, *Speech of William H. Seward*, 27–28.

Methodist Episcopal Church. His track record as an unyielding abolitionist led to his eventual removal by the General Conference. During these
years of editorship, he released his 1852 book, *The Higher Law, in Its Relations to Civil Government.*[61]

Hosmer's book began by honoring Seward but quickly moved to the
fundamental principles of law. He quoted the Declaration of Independence
with admiration and reiterated the purposes of government found in the
preamble to the United States Constitution. His argument imported brief
excerpts from French political philosopher Montesquieu but grounded
much of his advocacy in William Blackstone.

Hosmer was adamant that civil government could not create or restrict any of humanity's natural rights or powers. Rights are granted by
God, prior to any human legislation, and he readily affirmed the language
used for these rights in the Declaration of Independence (life, liberty, and
the pursuit of happiness). He reasoned, "So obvious indeed is this fact, that
Blackstone says, the civil law can neither take them away, nor by giving
them its sanction, add any thing to the authority by which we hold them.
They are just as much ours without, as with legislation—that is to say, they
are wholly beyond the reach of any law that man can make."[62] Once again
William Blackstone was enlisted in the cause of liberty.

Hosmer believed that the Scriptures, properly interpreted, supported these philosophical claims, but Southern contemporaries found
his perspective misguided and dangerous. This is not at all surprising,
but the way some defended slavery revealed much about their reading of
America's founding principles.

William Andrew Smith (1802–70) was one Southerner who mar-
shaled an array of biblical interpretations and philosophical arguments to
buttress slavery. Smith was born in Fredericksburg, Virginia, and became
a Methodist pastor in the middle 1820s. He served churches throughout
Virginia and blossomed into a preacher of great renown. He was a del-
egate to every General Conference of the Methodist Episcopal Church
from 1832 to 1844.[63]

In 1846 Smith was elected to the presidency of Randolph-Macon
College in Virginia, a Methodist institution. The same year that William
Hosmer was replaced as editor of the *Northern Christian Advocate* (1856)

---

61. Stilwell, "Rev. William Hosmer," 101.

62. Hosmer, *Higher Law*, 47.

63. Blackwell, "Smith," 361–62.

Smith published his *Lectures on the Philosophy and Practice of Slavery*. The college president was not above manipulating Scripture to endorse slavery, but he also wielded philosophical language to make his case.

As one observer has said, Smith labored to repudiate "the theory of natural rights developed in the Enlightenment."[64] He argued that inequality is the will of God and that a proper reading of the Bible came to this conclusion. Smith was especially vexed that the language of equality found its way into the Declaration of Independence. He could not conceal his disdain for this idea, which he attributed to "the infidel philosophy of France."[65] Today we treasure the principle of equality, even though it has not always been practiced. During William Andrew Smith's era, many judged the idea itself anathema.

Therefore, in the years leading up to our Civil War, the Methodist battle over slavery was fueled by various ideas and distortions of ideas. Among the day-to-day witness of Methodist folk, these foundational notions were not always articulated in explicit form or defined with precision. But such ideas were always present, nonetheless. The lives of Sojourner Truth, Luther Lee, Laura Haviland, Henry Bibb, and Gilbert Haven were not motivated by random impulse. They embodied, in diverse ways, core convictions about the nature and intended destiny of humanity. Such lives also unfolded against a backdrop of competing loyalties. Who would triumph in contention for their hearts and minds? How would they navigate conflicting claims of authority? How would they serve God and all of God's people?

64. Smith, "William Capers and William A. Smith," 31.
65. Smith, *Lectures on the Philosophy*, 66.

Chapter II

SOJOURNER TRUTH

The Law Is in Her Heart

I *Know* You, and I *Don't* Know You

ON APRIL 28, 2009, a bust was unveiled in Emancipation Hall at the United States Capitol. Such events are designed to be milestones. Placing a piece of public art in the Capitol is not an accidental act. It takes planning, coordination among elected officials, and wide-ranging popular support. This unveiling represented all of that—and more. The bust was a likeness of abolitionist Sojourner Truth.

The backstory to Truth's inclusion at the Capitol is symbolic and symptomatic of forces she challenged during her life. In 1997 a sculpture of three women's rights leaders was moved from an obscure location in the Capitol basement to the Rotunda. The three were Lucretia Mott, Susan B. Anthony, and Elizabeth Cady Stanton—all overlooked and underrated Americans who battled for equality. The three were also white and relatively privileged when compared to the struggles endured by women of color. The National Political Congress of Black Women, Inc. and others celebrated the recognition of women's rights but protested that a fourth individual belonged with the honored group—Sojourner Truth. More than ten years later, Truth found her place in Emancipation Hall.[1]

On one level, the placement of Sojourner Truth's likeness represented a victory. The bronze bust is the first sculpture to honor an African

---

1. Fulwood, "Black, White Feminists Are Caught Up."

American woman at the United States Capitol. The recognition marked a moment of arrival for all that Sojourner Truth represented. Yet on another level, the obstacles overcome during the placement process reminded astute observers of a hard reality. Sojourner Truth's inclusion was not automatic, and, while there was much to celebrate in her arrival, such moments are rarely given. They are, by necessity, taken. One might even be pardoned for wondering if Sojourner Truth would have been as impressed by the occasion as those lauding her. After all, Truth never measured herself by the pretensions of people with power, and she received inspiration and authority from beyond socially accepted norms (which, more often than not, excluded her). There may have been a little too much self-congratulation by political insiders on April 28, 2009.

None of this should surprise us. Sojourner Truth perseveres in death as she did in life. Isabella Baumfree (later, Sojourner Truth) was born sometime during 1797 in Ulster County, New York. Her parents, James and Elizabeth Baumfree, were enslaved on a farm in that region. This was the wild and majestic Hudson River Valley, north of New York City—not far from the Catskill Mountains. Truth's upbringing among this northern environment reminds us that slavery in America was not always a southern reality, with stereotypical Tidewater plantations and caricatured dialects. Slavery was a brutal commodification of people, in varied locales, up and down the Atlantic Seaboard.[2]

Truth's early childhood was spent with her youngest brother and parents as the legal property of Charles Hardenbergh, a Dutch farmer representing an especially well known dynasty of landowners. Earlier generations of the Hardenberghs embraced the pietism and heart religion of Theodorus Jacobus Frelinghuysen (1691–1747), a firebrand preacher from New Jersey's Raritan River Valley. Frelinghuysen led a spiritual revival during the early eighteenth century that was really a regional expression of America's First Great Awakening. His message and accessibility also appealed to disenfranchised white people, those who lacked the genteel contacts of established power. Interestingly, the Hardenberghs were extremely privileged, and so their affinity for Frelinghuysen's grassroots renewal ran counter to assumptions about class. Yet while Dutch pietism had populist appeal, it did not necessarily lead to egalitarian social

---

2. Washington, *Sojourner Truth's America*, 9–17.

convictions and practices. There were plenty of Frelinghuysen devotees who saw nothing wrong with slavery.[3]

The Dutch cultural context seeped into Sojourner Truth's life and had a lasting impact on her spiritual vision, but her mother's religious instruction was more powerful and formative. Elizabeth Baumfree would gather her children in the evening and talk of God. She knew that the divine maker was the only one who could protect her family, and she added, "My children, there is a God, who hears and sees you."[4] If hearing people to speech is a grace, then it begins with the one who created the very act of listening. God knew young Sojourner Truth and heard her. Because of this she found her voice.

At other times, Elizabeth would exclaim in the language of the Psalms, "Oh Lord, how long?"[5] She knew her children faced a demonic system that was engineered to grind them down. When would it end? According to later telling, Elizabeth also pointed to the stars and moon and said, "Those are the same stars, and that is the same moon, that look down upon your brothers and sisters."[6] Many of Elizabeth's children were torn away from her, but she always redirected herself and her remaining youngsters to view the world from God's perspective. Down here the pain was unbearable, but over all of creation was one who gathered sorrow into an inexhaustible heart.

The reality of God and the realms of worldly power were, thankfully, not the same. Sojourner Truth's world was a disgraceful parody of God's design and stood under the judgment of divine standards, but some day things would be different. She did not live in a place where detached reflection about God's law and human law was common. She did not work and negotiate an environment of formal debate regarding divine authority and human legislation. But she knew there was a yawning chasm between the intent of a loving God and the distortions of power all around her. Later, when Truth's son was sold away from her, she vowed to use the legal system to retrieve him. Margaret Washington wrote, "The secular rule of law, heretofore favoring slavery, would become a sacred weapon," making people "instruments of divine law."[7] Sojourner Truth lived as if she believed this.

3. Washington, *Sojourner Truth's America*, 18–31.
4. Truth, *Narrative of Sojourner Truth, a Northern Slave*, 17.
5. Truth, *Narrative of Sojourner Truth, a Northern Slave*, 18.
6. Truth, *Narrative of Sojourner Truth, a Northern Slave*, 18.
7. Washington, *Sojourner Truth's America*, 62.

In 1810 Truth became the legal property of John J. Dumont and moved to New Paltz, New York. She remained there until emancipating herself in 1826. Her first partner, Robert, was kept away by someone claiming to own him.[8] She then married a man named Thomas in 1820. Some recalled that the officiant was an African American itinerant Methodist.[9] But this union was burdened by a legal system that made marriage among enslaved people fragile and vulnerable. Most would say people thus united were not really married. For Sojourner Truth, this was upside-down thinking. If the worldly authorities did not recognize her marriage that was their problem. She knew that God held ultimate dominion.

In 1817 the state of New York passed a law emancipating all enslaved adults on July 4, 1827, provided they were born before 1799. Younger people would remain in bondage until they were twenty-five (if female) and twenty-eight (if male). The symbolism of July 4 was significant, and it conjured up notions of freedom in America's founding. It also highlighted the hypocrisy of slavery. Sojourner Truth struggled with what it meant to labor for another decade under inhuman conditions. As the time of emancipation approached, John Dumont promised that if she worked hard, he would free her and Thomas a year early. However, Dumont broke his word, and Truth made a monumental decision.[10]

On an autumn morning in 1826, Sojourner Truth took her baby Sophia and walked to freedom. She did not go far and found safety at the home of Isaac and Maria Van Wagenen, advocates for liberation. When John Dumont came calling, demanding her return, the Van Wagenens intervened. Contrary to their practice of never acknowledging human bondage, they purchased the remaining labor claimed by Dumont. Truth asked how she might address Isaac Van Wagenen, and he insisted that she not call him "master," adding, "there is but *one* master; and he who is *your* master is *my* master."[11] Truth finally found a white person who understood divine authority.

It must also be remembered that Truth's odyssey was not merely physical and geographical. To arrive at this point she traveled through several iterations of God-consciousness. Contemporaries observed a development in her soul and attempted to "trace the exercises of a human

8. Washington, *Sojourner Truth's America*, 52.

9. Washington, *Sojourner Truth's America*, 71.

10. Washington, *Sojourner Truth's America*, 51–56.

11. Truth, *Narrative of Sojourner Truth, a Northern Slave*, 43.

mind, through the trials and mysteries of life."[12] Such grandiloquent aims must be received with reservation, but Truth was, in addition to all else, a sojourner among the world of theological ideas.

The clear notions of God's supremacy and protection inherited from her mother were later given contour through audacious prayer. She found a safe place, a small island in the middle of a stream. Among large willows Sojourner Truth poured her heart out to the only one who seemed to listen with any compassion. She chose the spot for its natural splendor and because the sound of surrounding waters kept her words from being "overheard by any who might pass that way."[13] If hearing can give birth to speech, being heard by dangerous forces might bring disaster.

In hindsight, it appears that Sojourner Truth's blending of Dutch pietism and Methodism began while living with the Van Wagenen family. Her hosts were Reformed Christians, but they also attended the region's Methodist camp meetings.[14] Truth's spiritual growth during this time was opaque and eclectic.

Sometime in the spring of 1827, she had a premonition that John Dumont would attempt to take her back to slavery. Later she considered this a critical moment of temptation. The cultural celebrations around Pentecost were coming, with their fleeting expressions of indulgent behavior, and she wavered in her commitment to a new life. Perhaps living under the control of Dumont was not so bad if she could lose herself every now and then in wild revelry. Her *Narrative* describes this as a test resembling the biblical wavering of God's people following exodus. Just as those liberated through the Red Sea almost returned to the fleshpots of Egypt, Sojourner Truth considered submitting once more to John Dumont.[15]

When Dumont arrived at the Van Wagenen farm, Truth prepared to go with him. However, just as she was about to board his carriage "God revealed himself to her, with all the suddenness of a flash of lightening."[16] Sojourner Truth stood face-to-face with the creator of all that is, and the first impression was dramatic, or more accurately, traumatic. She became aware of her

12. Truth, *Narrative of Sojourner Truth, a Northern Slave*, 59.
13. Truth, *Narrative of Sojourner Truth, a Northern Slave*, 60.
14. Washington, *Sojourner Truth's America*, 70.
15. Truth, *Narrative of Sojourner Truth, a Northern Slave*, 64.
16. Truth, *Narrative of Sojourner Truth, a Northern Slave*, 65.

smallness and her sin, her doubting the one who had sustained her: "Oh, God, I did not know you were so big."[17] The experience was terrifying.

She walked back into the house and tried to resume some chores, but her soul would not rest. She felt exposed and broken. How confidently she had addressed God in her wilderness retreat. Now that familiarity seemed pretentious. How could she dare speak to her maker?

Then someone appeared to stand in the breach and represent her cause. Who was this? Who could do with such eloquence that which she was incapable of doing? "Who *are* you?" she begged and added, "I *know* you, and I *don't* know you."[18] An answer washed over her with divine clarity. The someone was Jesus, come to plead her case. Before she had considered Jesus a great person of religious importance, but now she knew him as a Savior. He "appeared to her delighted mental vision as so mild, so good, and so every way lovely, and he loved her so much!"[19] In fact, she was convinced that he had always loved her, even though she had never realized this glorious truth. The terror turned into gladness and gratitude. Sojourner Truth spent the rest of her life unpacking this vision, but something changed in her that day.

Margaret Washington concludes that Truth's experience of temptation, self-examination, and affirmation by Jesus represented her justification by grace through faith.[20] Justification names the gift of being considered righteous before God, despite brokenness and sin. In most traditions (especially the Methodist) it leads to growth in grace and becoming the person God designed one to be. This becoming is captured by the term sanctification, something that would live through Sojourner Truth's middle and later years. John Wesley held sanctification (sometimes called Christian perfection) as the signature teaching offered by Methodists to the world.[21] These twin doctrines (justification and sanctification) were not alien constructs foisted upon Truth's life. They were the spiritual rhythms that lived within her and radiated from her.

Among the archival holdings at the Bentley Historical Library in Ann Arbor, Michigan, is a scrap of paper relating to Sojourner Truth's conversion. It was penned for her on March 1, 1832, by a Methodist

17. Truth, *Narrative of Sojourner Truth, a Northern Slave*, 66.

18. Truth, *Narrative of Sojourner Truth, a Northern Slave*, 67.

19. Truth, *Narrative of Sojourner Truth, a Northern Slave*, 67.

20. Washington, *Sojourner Truth's America*, 74.

21. Wesley, "Letters to Robert C. Brackenbury, Esq.," 9.

pastor in Ulster County, New York. She carried this scrap within her carpetbag over the years, and it stood as a testimonial to her great change in 1827. The note reads, "It is now five years this winter since I knew there was a risen Saviour."[22] Perhaps the dating is a bit off. Truth's vision and transformation almost certainly happened in the late spring of 1827 and not during the winter, but the language is intriguing. What did she mean by knowing there was a risen Savior?

Theologians might strain to make sense of Sojourner Truth's awakening and how it related to an awareness of the resurrected Jesus. Because Truth did not read or write, the statement may reflect the word choice of that Ulster County pastor more than her intended description. This caution also applies when reading her *Narrative*, an account dictated by Truth to a friend. We cannot peel back the writing of her assistants completely, and we will never arrive at some pristine intent of Sojourner Truth. Readers are left to consider these concepts in their received form, and this dynamic is not unique to Truth's legacy. There are many ways to frame the meaning of her metamorphosis, and the murky points deserve attention. There were also more explicit, mundane issues at hand. For example, her transformation pointed to a change in day-to-day relationships.

The great confrontation, confession, and acceptance of 1827 led to inner freedom. Yet this liberation was intimately tied to her temptation and ultimate perseverance against the abuse of John Dumont. She did not go back to Egypt. She kept moving forward, and she found herself delivered from both paralyzing resignation and the demonic manipulation of others. She was now "free indeed" (John 8:36).

22. Bryant Lowe, Papers, MHC.

I Sell the Shadow to Support the Substance.

SOJOURNER TRUTH.

Sojourner Truth (1797–1883) sold photographs of herself to support her work.

Image Courtesy of the National Portrait Gallery,
Smithsonian Institution

The Lever of Truth

Around the time Sojourner Truth encountered Jesus, she toiled through a legal process to retrieve her son Peter. He had been torn away from her, and she vowed to have him back. For a while she lived in Kingston, New York, roughly fifteen miles north of New Paltz. Kingston was the county seat and center of legal deliberation. She eventually secured Peter's freedom, and the introduction to this region brought unanticipated changes in her life.

One day during the summer of 1827 Truth heard singing and prayer coming from a nearby house. She looked in the window and saw a small gathering of worshipers. They were Methodists, and they welcomed her. Soon she was a member of St. James Methodist Episcopal Church in Kingston.[23] Truth's affiliation with Methodism began through earlier attendance at camp meetings. It became more formal in Kingston. Her testimony regarding God's grace and protection meant something. She was asked to speak during worship services, and the story was compelling. Sojourner Truth became a preacher in her own right.[24]

If Truth's encounter with Jesus represented a justification by grace, her subsequent belonging to the Methodist movement represented a journey toward sanctification. In 1828 she moved to New York City. Her openness and willingness to work with a diverse range of people won her many friends, but she also remained rooted in the broad Methodist movement. A letter of transfer from the Methodist Episcopal church in Kingston paved the way for membership in New York's storied John Street Church. This congregation had been among the small pockets of pre-revolutionary Methodists in America. According to James Walker Hood (later bishop of the African Methodist Episcopal Zion Church) there was no original segregation or hierarchy of worshipers at John Street. People of African descent "were welcomed in common with other members to all the privileges of God's house and worship."[25] Sadly, this egalitarianism did not last.

Much like the overall Methodist witness regarding slavery, John Street Methodists began to mirror the values of their surrounding culture. Instead of mining theological truths for prophetic guidance, the congregation sought social acceptance. By the time Sojourner Truth joined the church, it had already become more stratified. Such facts remind us that many primal forms of Methodism did, indeed, live an admirable ethic—only to see it tragically compromised by yearnings for popularity in a racist world.

As the John Street Church became more status conscious, its moral witness waned. The search for social acceptance also created tensions with other unique Methodist emphases. John Wesley insisted that the desire for sanctification or Christian perfection remain a cardinal aim of

23. Washington, *Sojourner Truth's America*, 80.

24. Washington, *Sojourner Truth's America*, 80.

25. Hood, *One Hundred Years*, 1.

the movement. In polite society, this teaching was often misunderstood and considered a kind of fanaticism or unreasonable demand for purity. A denomination that lusted for social standing might think twice before making sanctification its signature emphasis. Therefore, during the early nineteenth century, as the Methodist movement enjoyed newfound popularity, several avoided a confrontation with slavery, while toning down the teaching on sanctification.

This shift did not mean that those who maintained a strong stand against slavery were automatically seeking sanctification, and many advocates for sanctification avoided the issue of slavery altogether. Yet there were some who saw abolition and sanctification as two sides of the same coin. For them, traditional Methodist teaching could never tolerate slavery.

When Sojourner Truth moved to New York City in 1828, she met James and Cornelia La Tourette—Methodists who desired to revive a focus on God's sanctifying power. The La Tourettes had recently left the John Street Church to lead a renewal movement. Truth was offered a job by the couple and began a period of domestic employment with them. For two years she moved between the established environment of John Street Methodist Episcopal Church and the enthusiastic home of the La Tourettes.[26]

By 1831 Truth joined the African Methodists and the congregation of Zion Church in New York.[27] It is difficult to gauge the impact various teachings regarding sanctification had on her overall witness, but for the rest of her life she demonstrated interest in Christian movements that stressed the perfectibility of people, communities, and even the nation. However, such pursuits did not always go well for her.

In May of 1832 Truth met the eccentric seer Robert Matthews (known as Matthias). The biblical figure Matthias had replaced Judas, and this self-styled disciple claimed to walk in the original's path—as if he was some type of reincarnation. Matthews asserted other outlandish prerogatives for himself and became a cult leader in Sing Sing, New York. To her later regret, Sojourner Truth fell for the enticing vision of spiritual life projected by Matthews.

Robert Matthews was born in 1788 among a Scottish Presbyterian family and became a carpenter. As a young man he was attentive and committed to his wife and children but became increasingly erratic over the years. Matthews neglected his work, preached on street corners,

---

26. Washington, *Sojourner Truth's America*, 83–84.
27. Washington, *Sojourner Truth's America*, 89.

interrupted conventional church services with judgmental tirades, and generally went off the deep end. He abandoned his family for weeks at a time while wandering near and far. Eventually, the mercurial prophet established a utopian community at the estate of wealthy merchants Ann and Benjamin Folger in Westchester County, New York.[28]

The colony was known as Zion Hill or Mount Zion (not to be confused with Zion Church, the African American congregation that supported Truth), and the commune had all the ingredients of other clandestine attempts at perfect living: moneyed benefactors (the Folgers), a mystical leader (Matthews), and a cast of odd and broken members. For reasons that are still the subject of debate, Sojourner Truth moved to Zion Hill.

She continued to work for little or no pay at domestic chores, and if Robert Matthews excelled at anything in life it was as an opportunist who took advantage of people. The misuse of power became so embedded among Zion Hill that it ceased to be observable by true believers. Traditional theological norms were dismissed as outmoded or even destructive to mature spirituality.

Like many other utopian ventures, Zion Hill ended up disregarding conventional understandings of marriage. Strange sexual relationships were endorsed and given religious support. People violated their marriage vows and engaged in sex with those declared "spirit spouses." The determiner of right and wrong in all matters was the unquestioned and authoritative Father Matthias (Robert Matthews). Before long, the community imploded under the weight of scandal and became a cautionary tale for those aspiring to perfection.[29]

In retrospect, Zion Hill represented a distortion of spiritual growth known as "antinomianism." Antinomianism (from the Greek, "against law") misused the idea of grace and excused licentiousness. According to this reasoning, if human law was subordinate to God's way, then special spiritual insight justified breaking all moral norms. Typically, such supposed insight belonged to a dictatorial leader. Destructive behavior was made to sound high minded, and the flaunting of convention always worked to the advantage of the self-described prophet.

Theologically speaking, antinomianism represented one of two dangers. The other was legalism, an obsessive devotion to worldly rules as if they came directly from God. In the early nineteenth century, many seeking

28. Washington, *Sojourner Truth's America*, 98–106.
29. Washington, *Sojourner Truth's America*, 106–26.

sanctification fell into legalism—a laborious attention to the tiniest details of moral behavior. Others went the opposite way, into antinomianism, substituting the arbitrary whims of a so-called leader for accepted norms. The debacle at Zion Hill was but one example of antinomian abuse.

During the fall of 1836, at the Oberlin Collegiate Institute in Ohio (later Oberlin College), students sought to understand the possibilities of sanctification. Their president, a philosopher named Asa Mahan (1799–1889), worried that they too would go down an antinomian road. However, Mahan offered a third way. Instead of grinding adherence to every dominant human rule (legalism) and instead of flaunting convention in destructive ways (antinomianism), the Oberlin president spoke of something he termed "the evangelical spirit."[30] This third perspective recognized God's law as supreme and sought to live it by grace.

There were certainly times when spiritually mature people had to confront worldly conventions, but the confrontation must come from a deep respect for God's law as revealed in Scripture. Authentic sanctification was never simply a pathological violation of norms but a principled honoring of God's intent for healthy and just relationships. Living this way was not achieved through striving; nor did it excuse arbitrary lusts and the misuse of power. Sanctification was only possible by grace, through faith—much like justification.

Viewed from the angle of biblical narrative, "the evangelical spirit" might be summed up with reference to Jer 31:33. God promised, "I will put my law within them, and I will write it on their hearts; and I will be their God, and they shall be my people" (NRSV). The established covenant was not to be discarded but renewed by grace and written on the human heart. There is little evidence that Sojourner Truth ever detailed her shifts in thinking regarding sanctification, but her life spoke volumes following the Zion Hill failure.

According to Truth's *Narrative*, she did considerable soul searching when the kingdom of Robert Matthews fell: "One thing she was sure of— that the precepts, 'Do unto others as ye would that others should do unto you,' 'Love your neighbor as yourself,' and so forth, were maxims that had been but little thought of by herself, or practised by those about her."[31] The judgment certainly holds for those at the top of the cult in Sing Sing. Such sentiments are probably too harsh when leveled at Sojourner Truth.

---

30. Mahan, *Scripture Doctrine of Christian Perfection*, 121–23.

31. Truth, *Narrative of Sojourner Truth, a Northern Slave*, 99.

In any event, she concluded that much of her time in and around New York City was wasted. This chapter of her life did not represent a genuine journey toward Christian sanctification.

During the early 1840s, Truth worked as a housekeeper in Manhattan for Perez and Lucy Whiting. The Whitings were shoemakers with hearts for justice. They trusted her and genuinely cared for her welfare. During the spring of 1843, Truth wrestled with her past and her uncertain future. She prayed much and sought direction from God. Finally, she received an answer. On June 1, 1843, she rose and made ready to leave the city. Lucy Whiting inquired about her intentions, and Truth replied that she was headed east. When Whiting responded with surprise, Truth added, "The Spirit calls me there, and I must go."[32] She also explained that she was taking a new name. Until that time, she had been known by names representing her experience in slavery or under sponsorship of friends: especially Isabella Baumfree or Isabella Van Wagenen. Henceforth and forevermore, she would be Sojourner Truth.

Many have referenced her day of departure, June 1, 1843, as Pentecost Sunday. In fact, the date fell on a Thursday. No matter. Sojourner Truth was beginning her third stage of life. Guided by the Spirit, she would not only focus on freedom or personal illumination. She was now on a mission—a mission for the benefit of others.

The change of name, of course, marked a dramatic transformation. Like Sarai who became Sarah, Abram who became Abraham, Saul who became Paul, something was radically different. Over the years, many have tried to deduce the exact meaning of the new name. This is dangerous work—as dangerous as the encounter with God that brought the name into being. Sojourner Truth would certainly have a nomadic quality to her life. She was on an extended journey. And her last name seemed to mean that her witness would shine light on the way things were and the way they ought to be. Yet beyond this, any certainty should be suspended. The precise meaning of her wandering and the reality she called out remain more than mystical, even to this day.

Once out of New York City, she wound her way through Long Island and then into New England. The year 1843 was also pivotal for a movement that anticipated the literal return of Christ. William Miller (1782–1849) was a Baptist pastor convinced that the Bible pointed to an imminent Second Advent. After propagating his beliefs in various forums,

32. Truth, *Narrative of Sojourner Truth, a Northern Slave*, 100.

he settled on a period between March 21, 1843, and March 21, 1844, as the time of return. Sojourner Truth received her divine summons in the middle of this pregnant moment.[33]

While Truth traveled east, she encountered varied revivals, many the result of social anxiety that came with William Miller's predictions. She worked within this culture, and later she would settle in a community dominated by Adventist thinking. But Sojourner Truth reckoned holy time differently. The Millerite excitement was rooted in a strict premillennialism—the conviction that Christ would return abruptly and usher in a thousand-year reign. Margaret Washington argues that Truth was a postmillennialist—believing that servants of God were called to pave a way for Christ before his return.[34]

Sojourner Truth's postmillennialist reading of history matched her newfound commitment to serve others. The quasi-hysteria that followed Miller's message fed on a pessimistic view of the world and its destiny. The arbitrary return of Christ might provide relief for the saved, but it hardly inspired steady, devoted work to improve society. Just as the cult of Robert Matthews excused destructive behavior in the name of some superior spiritual insight, the doctrines of William Miller could lead to lack of regard for others while awaiting cataclysm. Truth did not buy the frenzy and its potentially dismissive ethic.

About this time, an earnest soul in Bristol, Connecticut, wrote a note commending Truth's preaching. She carried it with her as a letter of introduction. The turn of phrase in this note revealed, perhaps unintentionally, the core of her mission. This man, Henry L. Bradley, advised that listeners to Truth should "let her tell her story without interrupting her, and give close attention, and you will see she has got the lever of truth, that God helps her to pry where but few can."[35] In closing, Brother Bradley insisted that "she cannot read or write, but the law is in her heart."[36] The moral law, the very law of God, was neither an external burden nor something to be discarded. Like the prophecy in Jer 31, the law was a living inspiration within the heart of Sojourner Truth.

---

33. See the classic account of William Miller's movement in Cross, *Burned-Over District*, 288–321.

34. Washington, *Sojourner Truth's America*, 153.

35. Truth, *Narrative of Sojourner Truth, a Northern Slave*, 106.

36. Truth, *Narrative of Sojourner Truth, a Northern Slave*, 106.

She Belongs to Humanity

Before dawn on August 17, 1847, at O'Dell's Mill in rural Cass County, Michigan, a battle was brewing. The site, some eleven miles north of the Indiana state line, on Christiana Creek, was to serve as a rendezvous for bounty hunters. Raiders from Kentucky had spread out to capture people escaping slavery. When they met up at the mill, with captives in tow, things did not go as planned. The thugs found themselves surrounded by an interracial group of local farmers determined to prevent any abductions. One William Jones, a local abolitionist, disarmed a raiding Kentuckian and forced another from his horse. Before more serious violence broke out, the group of kidnappers was made to walk to Cassopolis, the county seat. There a proper judge would decide the fate of both the invaders and the people they had abducted.[37]

The raiders had reason to believe that the court would find in their favor, allowing them to capture those fleeing slavery. After all, Article IV, Section 2 of the United States Constitution sanctioned the return of people escaping bondage. A law from 1793 strengthened this provision. However, the Cass County, Michigan Circuit Court Commissioner was absent on August 17, 1847, and nearby Berrien County Circuit Court Commissioner Ebenezer McIlvain took the case. McIlvain was an abolitionist and a conductor on the Underground Railroad. The Kentuckians were sent packing without any of the captured people.[38]

This and other confrontations were followed by demands from southerners that the so-called "fugitive" laws be given even greater specificity and teeth for enforcement. By 1850 a new Fugitive Slave bill was before the United States Congress. The bill became law (contained within the Compromise of 1850) and had the effect of nationalizing interests previously tolerated within certain states. Federal officials were enlisted to issue warrants for the return of people seeking freedom on the Underground Railroad, and there were penalties for citizens in the North who would not aid in capturing those leaving slavery. Additionally, federally appointed commissioners were paid ten dollars if they rendered a decision in favor of bounty hunters and kidnappers. They were paid five dollars if they found in favor of enslaved people.[39]

37. Mathews, *History of Cass County, Michigan*, 113.
38. Tucker, *Twenty-First Century History*, 17.
39. Green, *Politics and America in Crisis*, 19–43, 50.

During 1850, Sojourner Truth was living in Florence, Massachusetts—the northwestern section of greater Northampton, Massachusetts. A local colony of reformers had befriended her in the middle 1840s, and while that experiment was now defunct, she remained in the area. Northampton was the colonial home of legendary theologian and revivalist Jonathan Edwards (1703–58), bright light of the First Great Awakening. It was also the birthplace of Second Great Awakening evangelical reformers Arthur and Lewis Tappan. By the middle nineteenth century, Northampton hosted a disjointed assortment of egalitarians and genteel vacationers from the South. This region was important to Sojourner Truth for many reasons. On April 15, 1850, she purchased a house at 35 Park Street in Florence. The home was paid off during 1854, in part from sales of Truth's autobiography.[40]

The *Narrative of Sojourner Truth, a Northern Slave, Emancipated from Bodily Servitude by the State of New York, in 1828* was a cooperative work, dictated through the pen of Olive Gilbert (1801–84). Gilbert was born in Brooklyn, Connecticut, and raised as a Unitarian, under the preaching of Samuel J. May. By early 1850, Truth was already anticipating publication of her *Narrative*.[41] The two women made a good team—Truth the incisive advocate and organizer, Gilbert more pensive and literary. The *Narrative* was Sojourner Truth's story, channeled through the writing of Olive Gilbert. The publication was an autobiography, not a biography. Sojourner Truth's voice did not need to be in print for it to be heard, but when it did appear in writing, the voice still belonged to her.

Truth's expression was always mediated through the pen of others when it found itself on paper, and this has posed a challenge to posterity. For instance, her famous 1851 "Ain't I a Woman?" speech has been contested by commentators for years. Newspaper accounts of that address, along with several attempts at transcribing what was heard, have left generations unsatisfied. Whose recollection captured the essence of Sojourner Truth? How did cultural assumptions of the time distort the speech? If one peeled back the layers of memory, could one get to her exact words?

Such questions have a way of backfiring on us. Those who deconstruct various printed versions of this speech typically claim to be unleashing the real Sojourner Truth. But even these efforts manipulate more than they liberate. Attempts to reach the pure message presume that she requires someone else to free her. We should always remember that, even

40. "Stop #16: Sojourner Truth's House."

41. Washington, *Sojourner Truth's America*, 181–82.

though state law released Truth in 1828, she walked away from slavery on her own terms before then, and the only one who ever really freed her was the God who loved her.[42]

On April 26, 1850, the abolitionist newspaper *The Liberator* carried the following announcement: "JUST PUBLISHED, And for Sale at the Anti-Slavery Office, 21 Cornhill, NARRATIVE OF SOJOURNER TRUTH, a Northern Slave, Emancipated from Bodily Servitude by the State of New York in 1828. With a Portrait."[43] This very paper also contained blistering commentary aimed at the pending legislation in Washington that would nationalize the recapture of people leaving slavery. April 1850 was a critical month for Sojourner Truth. It marked the agency and self-determination that comes with being a homeowner, the premiere of her autobiography, and the ominous foreshadowing of so-called Fugitive Slave legislation. As her personal life became better established, the nation stumbled toward even more systematic oppression.

Frederick Douglass feared that any law mandating the nationwide pursuit of those escaping bondage would drive thousands on to Canada. He labeled the legislation the "Bloodhound Bill." When enacted in September of 1850, the new law served as an accelerant for the fire consuming America.[44] Many abolitionists referred to the act with disdain; they continued to call it the "Fugitive Slave Bill," even after it was signed. Nothing so contrary to the divine will could ever be termed a legitimate law.[45]

It made perfect sense for Truth's book to be advertised in *The Liberator*. Begun in 1831 by Boston's William Lloyd Garrison (1805–79), this publication became America's best-known abolitionist organ. Garrison was larger than life and not one to avoid controversy. He was also not one to minimize his own abilities. Garrison demanded immediate abolition of slavery and yet taught that political action to achieve this end sullied the moral authority of activists. He added some rather acerbic criticisms of the Christian church, too, which did not win him supporters among privileged religious figures. Garrison appointed himself a sponsor of many African American writers and abolitionists, and he took a particular interest in Sojourner Truth.

---

42. Malcom, "Does the Sojourner Truth Project."
43. "Just Published," 67.
44. Washington, *Sojourner Truth's America*, 196.
45. Dayton, *Discovering an Evangelical Heritage*, 47.

For her part, Truth received Garrison's assistance with grace. She had no stake in defending conventional institutions and so appreciated his prophetic indictment of the government and hypocritical churches. This did not mean that she agreed with all that Garrison said or with his pretentious invective, but she always responded to people according to their character and not with reference to their support for or judgment of official bodies. To call Sojourner Truth a bridge builder among antislavery people might suggest some intentional work in creating partnerships for action. She managed to do this but not as an implementation of strategy. Rather, she related to people on a personal basis, according to their authenticity, and sorted out the organizational details as she went along.

One friend of Truth's who presented a decided contrast to William Lloyd Garrison was the young pastor Gilbert Haven. Gilbert and Mary Haven moved from Amenia, New York, near the Connecticut state line to Northampton, Massachusetts, in 1851. Truth and the Havens developed a connection of souls that would extend beyond Mary's death in 1860 to Gilbert's passing in 1880.

When the Havens were appointed to a new charge in Wilbraham, Massachusetts, in 1853, they hired Truth's daughter, Diana, to work in their home.[46] The friendship was so strong that Haven defended Sojourner Truth as many establishment Methodists accused her of being a dangerous influence. A notice appeared in the New England paper *Zion's Herald* during 1855, warning Methodist congregations not to invite Truth into their pulpits. Haven was livid and responded in print that Truth had much to teach the church. Besides, he reasoned, she was not really a Garrisonian.[47]

This last claim bent the facts a bit. Sojourner Truth was closer to William Lloyd Garrison than Gilbert Haven liked to admit. However, she understood herself to be a Methodist, even if her denominational leaders did not always welcome her. Haven's defense may have revealed his own tumultuous relationship with church power as much as anything else.

By the middle 1850s, there were evident shifts in politics related to slavery, as well as shifts in Sojourner Truth's life. In January of 1854, Illinois senator Stephen Douglas introduced a bill in Congress that divided a huge tract of land west of Missouri. These territories would then be allowed to determine their status as slave or free states. The Missouri Compromise of 1820 required that these territories remain without slavery. Douglas and others

46. Washington, *Sojourner Truth's America*, 266–67.
47. Gravely, *Gilbert Haven Methodist Abolitionist*, 49.

desired to appease the South by reopening the limits of this earlier bargain. The Kansas-Nebraska Act was signed into law on May 30, 1854. Nebraska's status as a free state was not in doubt, but in Kansas, matters were up for grabs. Competing groups of "settlers" poured into Kansas and fought over whether the territory would enter the Union slave or free.

The drama in Kansas shifted much attention among the abolitionist movement from east to west. The fluid and turbulent nature of population growth and policy regarding slavery beyond the Mississippi River made that region a new battleground.

Sojourner Truth found herself pulled west during this time. At first her movement was subtle, as she continued speaking and organizing in places like western New York and Ohio. In October of 1856 Truth visited Battle Creek, Michigan, where she spoke to the Michigan Yearly Meeting of the Friends of Human Progress. This gathering, dominated by prophetic Quakers, appreciated her insights. She shared her vision of God and said, "Some years ago there appeared to me a form. Then I learned that I was a human being."[48] It was God who affirmed her humanity when the world said that she was not a person. Truth was embraced by activists in Michigan and liked the people. During July of 1857, she sold her home in Northampton and moved to Battle Creek.

At first Truth lived outside of Battle Creek, to the west some six miles, in yet another community of reformers. This one was called "Harmonia" and promoted peace and love, in contrast to the surrounding culture. However, the experiment at Harmonia, like most such utopias, did not last long. By 1860, financial troubles brought an end to the venture, and on August 4, 1862, as the Civil War was raging, a tornado swept through the village, destroying much of the property. In 1867 Truth moved to a house on 38 College Street in Battle Creek.[49]

The relocation to Battle Creek put Truth in touch with familiar movements and new friends. Many followers of William Miller and his premillennialism were settling there, and she reconnected with this community. Truth's appreciation for the Adventist movement has led many to claim that she held formal membership in this church while residing in Battle Creek, but the evidence is unclear. She lived from a collection of theological principles more than from official membership in any church body. Likewise, her

48. "Proceedings of the Annual Meeting," 4.
49. Buckley, "Rise and Fall of Harmonia."

appreciation for the Quaker tradition and especially her welcome by them in Battle Creek did not mean that she was no longer Methodist.

One Michigan abolitionist who grew close to Sojourner Truth was a gentle and fierce educator from Lenawee County named Laura Smith Haviland. Born a Quaker, she became a member of the egalitarian Wesleyan Methodists (a reform group that had left the Methodist Episcopal Church). When Haviland corresponded with Truth, she referred to her as "Sister Sojourner," and the two conspired after the Civil War, bringing relief to recently freed people.[50]

In 1865, Sojourner Truth and Laura Haviland found themselves in Washington, DC, working for the Freedmen's Bureau. One day, as they attempted to board a streetcar, a racist conductor tried to push Truth off and sneered at Haviland, demanding, "Does she belong to you?" Laura Haviland shot back, "She does not belong to me, but she belongs to Humanity."[51] Truth was not only a person; she had become a truly universal person. Belonging was not to be a possession of someone else but, rather, to be in relationship with each and all. Humanity was the beneficiary of her personhood. Sojourner Truth died on November 26, 1883, and is buried in Battle Creek, Michigan.

The years have witnessed an ironic honoring of Sojourner Truth, and these things are perhaps better late than never. The same person assaulted on a Washington, DC streetcar somehow ended up in Emancipation Hall of the United States Capitol—nearly one hundred and fifty years later. Truth's arrival was a testament to her staying power in public and moral imagination. It also exposed the resistance she endured during her earthly life. No one freed Sojourner Truth, and no one did her any favors by placing a bust in the Capitol. These events were belated recognition of something that was always there. Her value came from God, not the tardy affirmation of others. Her rights were created and then only imperfectly acknowledged. Sojourner Truth was known for her presence, but it was a presence grounded in the unmistakable authority of God.

50. Truth, *Narrative of Sojourner Truth, A Bondswoman*, 293.
51. Truth, "Truth, Sojourner, letter to Amy Kirby Post."

The Sojourner Truth Monument in Battle Creek, Michigan was dedicated in 1999.

Photo by Christopher P. Momany

Chapter III

LUTHER LEE

The Supremacy of
the Divine Law

A Practical Scholar

DURING THE LATE 1990s, an intriguing archaeological project at a Syracuse, New York, church caught the imagination of many. The study examined a group of sculpted clay faces that had been carved into the church's basement walls. When were these faces formed? Who sculpted them? Were they intended to depict someone in particular?

This building served as a home for the Wesleyan Methodist Church in downtown Syracuse. The structure, located on the corner of Onondaga and Jefferson Streets, was built in 1847, and during the 1850s the congregation became known as a hive of abolitionist activity. It also distinguished itself as a stop on the Underground Railroad. Because of its ties to the freedom movement, archaeologists were tantalized by the possibility that the carved faces were artwork left by those seeking shelter in the church basement. Mysterious clues of this nature are apt to set the imagination soaring. Did those seeking freedom really create this art? Were these faces eloquent, if earthy, signatures of courage and sublime principle?

The carefully excavated faces have been removed and preserved in a local museum, but the artists in question remain unconfirmed. The beauty of such a story is that it very possibly documents the previously overlooked creativity of those who traveled the Underground Railroad.

The caution within this story relates to unresolved questions. It cannot be said with certainty that those moving toward freedom created the carvings. The iconic pastor of the Syracuse Wesleyan Methodist Church would want our attention to remain focused on the tangible witness of those who made the journey, and his advocacy only adds to the case for concluding that the artwork came from people seeking liberty. That pastor was named Luther Lee (1800–1889), and his witness for justice, as well as theological rationale for the movement, inspired many.[1]

By the time Rev. Luther Lee arrived in Syracuse, he was already a phenomenon on the abolitionist circuit. From humble origins, he developed a reputation for biting critique of slavery. An intense determination, firm countenance, and deep-set eyes accompanied his rapid-fire oratory. They called him "Logical Lee," owing to his habit of stringing together tight arguments whenever engaged in debate. Not shy about stating his views, he backed them up with surprising erudition for one not formally educated.

Lee was born in Schoharie, New York, on November 30, 1800. His father, Samuel Lee, served in the American Revolution. His mother, Hannah Williams Lee, lost the support of family as a child. She was subsequently raised in the home of revered New England divine Joseph Bellamy. Samuel and Hannah Lee had nine children, Luther being next to the youngest.[2]

Soon after Luther Lee's birth his family moved to Delaware County, New York, more specifically to Kortwright Township. Here the youngster became acquainted with the legendary Bangs family of Methodist tradition. Rev. John Bangs was especially prominent as an early religious influence on the boy and even preached at the Lee home. Later, Luther Lee would remember Bangs for his "very loud and earnest exhortation." In 1809 the family relocated once more to Ulster County, New York.[3]

Ulster County was the birthplace of Sojourner Truth some twelve years earlier, but the connection with Luther Lee was more geographic than real. Lee lost his mother, Hannah, when thirteen years old, and his father Samuel died the following year. This grief left an indelible, practical imprint on his life. The family was split up, and the teenage Luther Lee found himself alone in the world, with God as his sole guide and few others in his corner. He

1. Armstrong and Wurst, "Clay Faces in an Abolitionist Church," 19–37.
2. Lee, *Autobiography*, 15–17.
3. Lee, *Autobiography*, 17.

headed northwest along the Old Esopus Turnpike, over Hemlock Mountain, and landed in Middletown, Delaware County, New York.[4]

At Middletown he worked for a man named Smith who owned a gristmill. Luther Lee became a principal part of Smith's business operation, until the fall of 1817, when he went to work for a tanner, Daniel H. Burr. Burr was an honest man who treated Lee fairly, but he was a Deist. Lee resolved to make up his mind regarding religious questions. As a child, his mother had read to him from the narrative of Methodist evangelist and abolitionist Freeborn Garrettson, but the supportive maternal influence ended with her death. Now, as a young man, Lee had to draw his own theological conclusions—and draw them he did.[5]

Luther Lee determined that God was no distant force or imperial first cause. God got involved in the world on behalf of humanity—loved each and all and expected them to live justly. At the age of nineteen he was baptized and joined the Methodist Episcopal Church. Lee's faith blossomed despite the generally skeptical character of his surroundings. His commitment was not perfunctory. Quite the opposite. Later he recalled, "That was an epoch in my life, a turning-point, the beginning of a brighter future."[6] The change came after hard-headed reflection and the exercise of an independent spirit. These qualities would serve him well as the years unfolded.

This reorientation of Lee's life was equally one of mind and heart. Many Christians from the period could tell of emotional crises that were resolved by the reception of God's love, and Lee certainly shared in this pattern of renewal. Yet he also described his conversion as a time of mental awakening—a vibrant exploration of thought and cognitive possibilities. He never disparaged the head while emphasizing faith. In fact, he recalled that the whole transformation was an episode in being "roused to greater mental activity."[7]

With new church associations, encouragement, and counsel Lee slowly discovered his gift for preaching. It may seem ironic given his later pulpit prowess that he began as a rather insecure proclaimer of the word. His confidence in God was robust, but he was haunted by a lackluster education. As a youngster an older brother cut the alphabet into a pine shingle with a penknife to teach him his letters. Beyond that, Lee struggled through youth and early adulthood to find a book here and there for self-improvement.

4. Kaufman, "Logical" Luther Lee, 12–13.

5. Kaufman, "Logical" Luther Lee, 12–13.

6. Lee, Autobiography, 21.

7. Lee, Autobiography, 22.

Fortunately, the same brother secured for him the *American Spelling Book*, and he slowly began to read the Bible and hymn book.[8]

Lee plugged away at his learning while preaching on the local Methodist Episcopal circuit. In 1823 he left Delaware County and its raw, rugged scenery for points farther north and west. At Plymouth, in Chenango County, he continued preaching, and the move broadened Lee's horizons in more ways than one. Here he met Mary Miller, a thoughtful and well-educated schoolteacher. After two years of courtship, they were married. Mary Miller contributed a great deal to Lee's continued learning, and he credited her with helping him overcome earlier deficiencies.[9] Some might describe Luther Lee as a self-made person, but this characterization is incorrect. He benefited mightily from the influence and insight of strong women—especially his mother and then Mary Miller. Lee would go on to champion the gifts and abilities women bring to the highest offices of Christian ministry, and he perhaps engaged in such advocacy because of his own powerful experience.

In 1827 Luther Lee received a recommendation for membership in the Genesee Annual Conference of the Methodist Episcopal Church. He was embraced on trial after spending some six years as a local preacher. This represented a step toward the more professional standing of formally trained Methodist clergy, but the next two years proved a grueling test. Lee traveled hundreds of miles as a stalwart itinerant preacher. He formed friendships with established Methodist clergy and generally got on well. He worked at balancing his vocation and commitment to a growing family, and, every now and again, he engaged in theological debate with rival preachers.[10]

Finally, in 1829, he became a candidate for ordination as a deacon. The examining committee of the annual conference looked him over and balked. They found his scholastic preparation lacking and reported him unfit for advancement. Fortunately, others had recently heard Lee preach and knew that his intuitive grasp of the gospel and natural genius qualified him in ways that were not easily apparent. He became a deacon and studied even more. He purchased a text in natural philosophy and one in rhetoric. He secured Buck's *Theological Dictionary*. Later Lee recalled, "If I could not be a classical scholar, with the polish and degrees of a collegiate

---

8. Lee, *Autobiography*, 25–26.

9. Lee, *Autobiography*, 28.

10. Lee, *Autobiography*, 30.

course, I could be a practical scholar in fact."[11] He was well on his way to becoming "logical" Luther Lee.

Before long, in De Peyster, New York, Lee found himself tangling with those who taught Universalism—the doctrine that all people are eventually saved. Followers of John Wesley preached that Christ did indeed die for every person, but this did not mean all would respond to the sacrifice. A carefully defined freedom, enlivened by grace, distinguished Methodists from Universalists. While God in Christ offered salvation to all, humans were accountable for receiving this gift. Luther Lee came into his own when he considered such matters and debated the Universalists of upstate New York.

The drama in De Peyster did not occur in a vacuum. A meeting house, built by the whole community, was to be dedicated for use by several different congregations. Because the Universalists and the Methodists were numerically strong in that area, the two groups would contribute a preacher for the dedication. Luther Lee was asked to represent the Methodists, and after drawing straws, he preached first. Despite his later reputation for disputatious sermonizing, by all accounts, Lee's message on this occasion exuded diplomacy. When his Universalist colleague stepped into the pulpit, a more confrontational spirit ruled. The contrasts between the two traditions could no longer be avoided. Lee announced that he would issue a response that evening. Word of the impending address swept the countryside, and a large crowd turned out. Luther Lee gave it to the Universalists without nuance, and his opponents issued a challenge to formal debate.[12]

The appointed contest took place a month later. The Universalists put forward the question, "Will all men be finally holy and happy?"[13] Because Lee's opponents introduced the question, they should have led the debate, but they would not. Lee ended up at a disadvantage, speaking first regarding a question he had not proposed. This dynamic allowed the Universalists to hear their adversary and then issue a host of counterarguments that fit their original assertion. However, Lee responded with his own cunning strategy. As the cycle of speaking continued, he used but one-third of his allotted time in rebutting the Universalists and took the offensive for the remaining minutes. The tables were turned, and by the end of the contest Wesleyan theology held the day. Unfortunately for the Universalists, some

11. Lee, *Autobiography*, 73–74.

12. Lee, *Autobiography*, 83–85.

13. Lee, *Autobiography*, 86.

supporters arrived at the debate inebriated. The drunken behavior did nothing to strengthen their case.[14]

Luther Lee was ordained an elder at the annual conference of 1831 and continued to serve a series of charges. At Antwerp in Jefferson County, New York, Lee experienced his last formal debate with the Universalists. He began writing for newspapers on the subject and later remembered, "I soon found I was as good a match for my opponent with the pen as I was in oral debate."[15] In 1836 he published a three hundred page book refuting Universalism. The accomplished preacher emerged a recognized author.

The year 1836 also proved momentous in the story of American Methodism's confrontation with slavery. Some clergy had expressed openly abolitionist convictions, and this did not go down well when the General Conference met in Cincinnati that May. The bishops and several in strategic positions engineered a gag rule, barring discussion of slavery and chastising those who advocated for freedom. While ostracized and marginalized, Orange Scott of New England carried the flag for abolitionists who would not capitulate. He had burst onto the scene in 1835 and was not about to avoid the awful truth. Soon, the moral conflict broke in on Luther Lee, and when it came, it roared as an overwhelming storm.[16]

Lee was serving a church in Fulton, New York, when confronted with the horrors of human bondage. Most considered the Fulton charge a fine appointment, but far from a place of privilege that avoided controversy, it lived as a community of conscience. Luther Lee settled in and found that many of his parishioners were already engaged in antislavery work. Our memory is accurate in appreciating Lee as a leader of the fight against slavery, but the facts demonstrate that he himself was led to self-examination and commitment by his people.[17]

Lee had followed the founding of the American Antislavery Society in 1833 and the assault on that organization's president, Arthur Tappan. A mob attacked Tappan's home, threw his furniture in the street, and burned it. Lee also noted that several people of color were targeted in and around New York City. He condemned this violence, but he could not really claim those days as a personal turning point. Until 1836/1837 he was more concerned with mob violence than with the moral imperative of abolition.[18]

14. Lee, *Autobiography*, 86–87.
15. Lee, *Autobiography*, 118.
16. Matlack, *Life of Rev. Orange Scott*, 85–107.
17. Lee, *Autobiography*, 133.
18. Lee, *Autobiography*, 133.

Then Lee watched the drama in Cincinnati during 1836, and he possessed a ringside seat to events which followed. Bishop Elijah Hedding presided over the annual conference that met in Potsdam, New York, during 1837. Lee heard Hedding's pathetic attempt to enlist the Golden Rule as a defense for slavery and later wrote that he was absolutely "cloyed"—which meant that he was sickened by the spectacle. The pastor could hardly hold his tongue, his pen, and his very person in check. He was at the boiling point.[19]

Understanding the motivation for change is a slippery task. Precipitating events often push one over the edge and into a new world of action. That is precisely what happened to Lee, but these crises also tend to come at the end of smaller, incremental changes. Pressure builds within until the energy is let out, often by a cataclysm of some kind. When Luther Lee became an open abolitionist, few were probably surprised. He had the temperament for such work: a razor-sharp mind, focus, and the determination to act on his convictions. But the catalyst for his advocacy arrived like a thunderbolt in the night.

Luther Lee (1800–1889) combined philosophical ideas with Scripture to attack slavery.

Image Courtesy of the Huguenot & New Rochelle Historical Association,
New Rochelle, New York

19. Lee, *Autobiography*, 135–36.

A Violation of Natural Rights

On the evening of November 7, 1837, a proslavery mob surrounded a building near the banks of the Mississippi River in Alton, Illinois. Winthrop Gilman's warehouse held a printing press that had been delivered earlier in the day, and the new machinery was under armed guard. The printing works belonged to abolitionist newspaper editor Elijah P. Lovejoy (1802–37). Lovejoy was a Presbyterian pastor with a heart for human rights, and this was his fourth press. Earlier equipment had been destroyed by proslavery marauders.

The mob that surrounded Lovejoy and some compatriots at Gilman's warehouse attempted to set the building on fire. Supporters of Lovejoy reacted with gunfire. A few moments later Lovejoy stepped out of the building and was shot five times. His death sent shock waves across America.

Luther Lee later recalled the news of Lovejoy's murder: "I was stirred, and judged it wrong to remain silent any longer."[20] He responded with a sermon that catapulted him into the middle of the abolitionist movement: "On the Occasion of the Death of the Rev. E. P. Lovejoy." The address was, of course, not a departure in terms of its relentless logic and energy, but its subject matter and the specific reasoning marked a turning point.

Preached to his Fulton congregation on Sunday, December 3, 1837, we might be forgiven for wondering how such a localized message could leave a widespread legacy. However, like notable sermons from others, this one by Lee was reprinted and received extensive coverage. It established his credentials as a bona fide abolitionist orator—with something unique to say, and the emphases of the sermon reveal much about Lee's particular approach to slavery.

For starters, Lee's homage to Lovejoy was shaped by the gruesome circumstances of the latter's death. He took as his text Acts 19:38, a somewhat obscure reference to the function of civil law in the face of mob violence. This chapter of Scripture tells the tale of Paul's ministry in Ephesus. The apostle challenged the cult of the goddess Artemis (or Diana). Because many Ephesian craftspeople earned a living by fashioning silver goods for this cult, they resented Paul's meddling. A hostile mob gathered to threaten Paul and his associates, and just as tensions were about to explode, a community official addressed the crowd. This leader reminded the mob that taking matters

---

20. Lee, *Autobiography*, 137.

into their own hands was unacceptable. If they had a complaint against Paul, there was a formal legal process to resolve such disputes.

The parallels between Paul in Ephesus and Elijah Lovejoy in Alton were obvious. Luther Lee built much of his sermon on the analogy and argued not so much for Lovejoy's position as for his right to speak his mind. Lee proclaimed, "The question is not, are abolitionists right? but have they rights?"[21] This made the sermon a defense of free speech, which was certainly needed, and to this day Lovejoy is remembered as a martyr for the free press. However, the rightness of his abolitionist commitment can be overlooked in such an approach.

Lee's sermon managed to include a direct condemnation of slavery, but the address focused on an analogy from Scripture that emphasized good civil law. The mob in Alton did violate the rudiments of public order, but what happens when the civil law itself undermines the law of God? Lee was not yet prepared to answer this question. It would be another ten years before he clarified the distinction between civil and divine authority. The sermon preached following Elijah Lovejoy's death did not express Lee's mature position, but it was a critical step forward.

Following Lee's dramatic support for abolitionists, he gained notoriety. His name was added to those who felt an increasing pressure from the Methodist Episcopal hierarchy. The bishops wanted to quell all controversy; it threatened to split a church that extended from Maine to the deep South. In 1838 Lee defended colleagues who were charged with exacerbating the conflict. While apologists for slavery suggested that it was not always wrong in practice, Luther Lee insisted, "I will plant my argument on the rock of eternal justice and on the God-given and inalienable rights of humanity, by denying that slavery can be right in any circumstances."[22] The Scriptures shaped his witness, but he was not beyond invoking natural rights.

Lee became a traveling antislavery speaker and confronted mobs of his own. When followers of William Lloyd Garrison eschewed political action in the fight against slavery, Lee responded by advocating for vigorous civic participation. He later recalled, "I was never utopian enough to give any quarter to non-resistance, or to suppose that humanity can exist in social relations without civil government; or that we can secure a right government without right voting."[23] Caught between those who insisted that the

21. Lee, *Five Sermons and a Tract*, 26.
22. Lee, *Autobiography*, 146.
23. Lee, *Autobiography*, 217.

government should protect slavery and those who gave up on government, Luther Lee joined others in charting a third way.

This was no compromise, either. It was as unyielding as Garrison, while remaining convinced that proper government could and absolutely must outlaw bondage. In the presidential election of 1840, Lee threw his energy behind the emergent Liberty Party—a radical antislavery movement that embraced political action.

The closing months of 1840 also marked an ominous development among the Methodist Episcopal Church. Proslavery forces within the denomination were bent on rooting out all abolitionists. Luther Lee continued his work for justice, but his position, as that of some others, was becoming more tenuous. During the fall of 1842, he accepted a summons to preach at the Methodist Episcopal Church in Andover, Massachusetts. The congregation had difficulty holding a pastor, given their staunch antislavery views, and Lee found a home, at least for a time.[24]

In October of 1842, Orange Scott, New England Methodism's leading abolitionist, held a small meeting with colleagues contemplating secession from the M. E. Church. The principal leaders of this impetus came from New England and New York State, and they resolved to organize a new denomination according to antislavery doctrine. Lee got wind of the gathering after the fact, but he soon joined the effort and became an advocate for the proposed "Wesleyan Methodist Connection of America." The movement was not confined to the East. A similar collection of Wesleyan voices for change had been at work in Michigan for nearly two years.[25]

The new church was organized formally at a conference held in Utica, New York, on May 31, 1843. Precisely one day before Sojourner Truth answered the Spirit's call and left New York City, a Wesleyan abolitionist denomination was born.

During the spring of 1844, the Methodist Episcopal Church split over slavery into northern and southern branches. Given this monumental breakup, one might wonder if the Wesleyan Methodists should have persevered for another year before founding a new denomination. But things were not that simple. History has given rise to a sunny narrative which portrays the post-1844 northern expression of the Methodist Episcopal Church as strongly antislavery. This was not entirely the case. The

24. Lee, *Autobiography*, 234.
25. Lee, *Autobiography*, 237–40.

movement that Luther Lee and his colleagues shaped offered a much more consistent abolitionist witness.

Lee served in Syracuse, New York, following the creation of the new denomination and wrote frequently for *The True Wesleyan*—a paper begun by Orange Scott that became the official organ of the Wesleyan Methodist Connection. During October of 1844 the fledgling church held its first General Conference in Cleveland, Ohio. Luther Lee was elected president of this body and appointed to serve as editor of *The True Wesleyan*. The paper was moved from Boston to New York, where Luther and Mary Lee lived for several years.

It was while engaged as editor that Lee preached another sermon destined for memory among the antislavery cause. Like his address following the death of Elijah Lovejoy, this one came after the death of an abolitionist martyr: Charles Turner Torrey (1813–46). Torrey was a Congregational pastor from Massachusetts who aided the escape of enslaved people in Washington, DC and Maryland during the early 1840s. He was arrested in Baltimore in June of 1844 and sentenced to six years of hard labor. Torrey died in 1846 from tuberculosis, while in prison.

His body was returned to Boston for burial, and Elijah Lovejoy's brother, Joseph (1805–71), preached the funeral sermon. Sometime during the spring of 1846 Luther Lee celebrated the life of Torrey in a sermon of his own titled "The Supremacy of the Divine Law." This address presented Lee's mature position regarding the relationship between civil government and God's authority, and he built upon the venerable higher law tradition. A third Lovejoy brother, Owen (1811–64), had preached a sermon by the very same title in January of 1842. Higher law thinking was becoming a common part of the abolitionist landscape.

The contrast between Lee's earlier sermon following mob violence in Alton, Illinois, and this one honoring Torrey is striking. Both addresses were grounded in biblical texts from the Book of Acts. The first sermon referenced good civil law highlighted in Acts 19:38. After Torrey's death Lee referenced Acts 23:29 and the way the apostle Paul's preaching was exonerated, even though it broke established human law. This logic of exoneration was then applied to the case of Charles Torrey. Torrey may have violated human codes, but these were not equal to the law of God. Accordingly, Lee's 1846 sermon shifted from a contemplation of good civil law to the preeminence of divine law.

Lee believed that Acts 23 demonstrated the way God's law stands above all human legislation, but he also relied on sources outside the Bible to make his case. Like John Wesley's "Thoughts upon Slavery," Lee's sermon did not limit itself to the Scriptures. It included a consideration of philosophically derived natural rights. He confessed, "My own standard is the Bible, but for the sake of the argument, I am willing to appeal to other standards."[26] He then quickly pointed to the American Declaration of Independence.

Lee understood this modern document to uphold "the rights of universal humanity."[27] Such rights are disclosed in the divine law: "The design of divine law is to reveal or make known to man what is right; the design of human law is to secure what is already known to be right."[28] Thus human law exists to mirror God's law. Human law does not in any manner create a difference between right and wrong; it is responsible for implementing God's prerogative regarding such matters. Lee applied this framework to Charles Torrey's activism and responded to those who accused Torrey of being rash or lacking in discretion: "In a word, his rashness and indiscretion were the result of the standard of virtue which he had adopted, which *dares to do right!*"[29] Unlike Lee's earlier sermon, this one not only considered rights (such as free speech and a free press), but the sermon given following Charles Torrey's death placed greater emphasis on that which is eternally right according to divine authority.

This argument had implications for the basic obligations of civil government. Four years later Lee watched in disbelief as Congress passed the Fugitive Slave provisions of 1850. Given the way Lee articulated a distinction between divine and human law, he was prepared to resist the new measures with all his heart. Moreover, his editorship at *The True Wesleyan* gave him a prime platform for blasting the legislation.

Lee eviscerated the 1850 law through a series of editorials titled "The Fugitive Slave Law: Its Unconstitutionality." These essays relied on his basic analysis of divine and human law, and he openly emphasized Enlightenment notions of human rights. Yet he also made a more technical argument that the Fugitive Slave legislation was not constitutional.

This critique drew from a school of interpretation known as "antislavery constitutionalism." In short, most Americans conceded that the United

26. Lee, *Five Sermons and a Tract*, 45.
27. Lee, *Five Sermons and a Tract*, 45.
28. Lee, *Five Sermons and a Tract*, 52.
29. Lee, *Five Sermons and a Tract*, 54 (emphasis original).

States Constitution tolerated slavery. Proslavery zealots even claimed that the Constitution clearly supported their view. On the other hand, those against slavery often wanted nothing to do with the Constitution. Luther Lee joined a third movement of those who claimed that, properly understood, the Constitution did not sanction slavery. This was by no means the dominant interpretation on either side of the slavery debate, but it had a cadre of eccentric and, at times, incisive advocates.

Writing in *The True Wesleyan* on October 26, 1850, Lee thundered that the Fugitive Slave law was "clearly a violation of natural rights and repugnant to the feelings of enlightened humanity."[30] This was the same argument he expressed some years earlier. However, Lee took these opening statements and developed a painstaking rebuttal of slavery, based on the principles of antislavery constitutionalism. First, he claimed that the euphemistic language of the Constitution never describes enslaved people as they were understood in 1850. The Constitution referred to persons "held to service," but just who such people were might be debated.[31] The drafters of the instrument may well have intended to describe enslaved people, but these possible or even probable intentions are not legally binding. Only the ratified language of the Constitution itself is law. This was a cardinal rule of antislavery constitutionalists.

On November 2, Lee argued that the Constitution never gave Congress undisputed authority to legislate regarding enslaved people from different states. In a rather ironic poke at those who tried to justify slavery through "states' rights," Lee suggested that federal power was indeed very much restricted regarding the escape or return of enslaved people. If his opponents wanted to stress the "rights" of states, they would have to accept the limitations placed on Congress regarding this matter.[32] On November 9, Lee cited the Fifth Amendment's provision that people not be "deprived of life, liberty, or property, without due process of law."[33] These were simply three of the many arguments Lee brought to bear on the subject, and his editorials almost certainly tired the most concentrated minds. But his dogged advocacy for the enslaved was nonetheless impressive.

From our vantage point, antislavery constitutionalism may seem like a lot of convenient hairsplitting employed to oppose the 1850 legislation, but

---

30. Lee, "Fugitive Slave Law," *True Wesleyan*, 8:43, 170.

31. Lee, "Fugitive Slave Law," *True Wesleyan*, 8:43, 170.

32. Lee, "Fugitive Slave Law," *True Wesleyan*, 8:44, 174.

33. Lee, "Fugitive Slave Law," *True Wesleyan*, 8:45, 178.

these theoretical arguments supported an activist commitment. Because Lee did not discard the Constitution, he was able to embrace civic life. Because he did not believe that slavery was constitutional, he was able to frame his advocacy as a patriotic adherence to good government.

The finer distinctions among Lee's thinking might not interest those pressing on toward God's justice, but the various pieces of his human rights vocation fit together. Logical Luther Lee was nothing if not consistent, and those who took the time to read or listen had much to consider.

The Scriptures Are the "Higher Law"

Within two years of writing his essays against the so-called Fugitive Slave law, Luther Lee resigned his position as editor of *The True Wesleyan* and returned to parish ministry. During the spring of 1852 he prepared himself to serve the Wesleyan Methodist congregation in Syracuse, New York. This church was no stranger to Lee; he helped form the congregation back in 1843. The church's building that stood on the corner of Onondaga and Jefferson Streets had been built while Lee lived in New York City. Now he moved into a house at 39 Onondaga Street and began three very fruitful years of ministry in Syracuse.

The arrival of the Lees in Syracuse took place the same year that Harriet Beecher Stowe published *Uncle Tom's Cabin*—perhaps the most significant piece of popular abolitionist literature before the Civil War. That year also witnessed the publication of William Hosmer's book *The Higher Law, in Its Relations to Civil Government*. Hosmer was then living in Auburn, New York, some forty miles west of Syracuse. These were explosive times, and central New York State distinguished itself as ground zero for politically active abolitionism.

The period that Luther and Mary Lee spent in Syracuse coincided with their most prolific work on the Underground Railroad. Later, Lee remembered this time: "I passed as many as thirty slaves through my hands in a month."[34] Assisting one enslaved person nearly every day of the year kept him busy, but he also managed to develop a warm relationship with his parishioners. While serving in Syracuse, Lee was called on to lead meetings related to several justice causes, and he preached regularly—sometimes traveling to address other congregations.

34. Lee, *Autobiography*, 331.

One such preaching assignment came as a particular honor and responsibility. Lee was invited to preach the ordination sermon for Antoinette Brown (1825–1921). Brown was a graduate of Oberlin College and had continued her training in theology at the school. During the early 1850s, she was approached to serve as the pastor at a Congregational church in South Butler, New York—located almost midway between Syracuse and Rochester. The community began planning for her ordination. Typically, such events featured the preaching of a respected member from one's own denomination, but Brown and her congregation sought out Luther Lee. The service took place on September 15, 1853, and Antoinette Brown is remembered as the first woman ever ordained by an established church body in America.

Lee's text for the ordination service was drawn from Gal 3:28: "There is neither male nor female; for ye are all one in Christ Jesus" (KJV). This remains a common reference for those who understand human relationships in terms of absolute equality, but Lee's affirmation of Brown also expressed a unique theology. In closing he addressed the very meaning of ordination.

Lee considered ordination to be a solemn rite, but he also knew it to be a human act. It does not create the legitimacy of pastors; it acknowledges God's prerogative to call pastors. The ordination of Brown honored the way she was "authorized, qualified, and called of God to preach the gospel of his Son Jesus Christ."[35] Essentially, Lee's proclamation mirrored his political philosophy. Like human rights, ordained ministry was not subject to the approval of powerful people. It was created by divine authority.

Lee's advocacy for women does not fit the assumptions of today's historians. When clergy abolitionists broke with William Lloyd Garrison in 1839, they did so, in large part, because they advocated political action. Yet a second issue emerged in the split. While many theologically traditional abolitionists entered the political fight on behalf of enslaved people, several did not support women's leadership. Followers of Garrison, who avoided politics, were generally more affirming of women—and less committed to orthodox theology. Luther Lee did not belong in either of these two camps. His theology was traditional, from a Wesleyan point of view, and he embraced political abolitionism. He was also more open to female leadership than most political abolitionists and even challenged his friend Orange Scott on behalf of women.[36]

---

35. Lee, *Five Sermons and a Tract*, 99.

36. Kaufman, *"Logical" Luther Lee*, 87–89, 166.

During his years in Syracuse Lee continued to write against slavery. By 1855 he released his book *Slavery Examined in the Light of the Bible*. The title suggests a straightforward treatment, but with Luther Lee, things were always a bit more complicated. For instance, the very first page claims that "the Scriptures are the 'higher law.'"[37] This statement unites two moral standards that some considered distinct sources of authority. The Scriptures were necessary for many who invoked a divine law in opposition to civil law, but others deemed the Bible an entirely different kind of measure.

Proslavery apologist William Capers claimed that the Scriptures were superior to any philosophical notions of a higher law, and he asserted that the Bible supported human bondage. When making this argument, he attempted to portray philosophical attacks on slavery as dangerously secular propaganda.[38] On the other side, abolitionists who tired of such appeals to Scripture often grounded their arguments in some different authority. Boston's Theodore Parker waxed eloquent regarding a higher standard of justice that condemned slavery, but he demonstrated little concern for orthodox theological convictions.[39]

Once again, Luther Lee did not fit the stereotypes. As a traditional Christian, he embraced the Scriptures. As an abolitionist, he believed that the Bible affirmed human rights. Here, as in other writings, Lee blended Enlightenment insights with biblical authority. This was especially the case when he invoked the Declaration of Independence and the teaching of Acts 17:26—all in one sentence. He insisted that to deny equality was to "deny the truth of the Declaration of American Independence" and to "disprove the unity of human nature, that 'God has made of one blood all nations of men,' equal in natural rights."[40] Others might drive a wedge between the Scriptures and the best of modern philosophy. Not Luther Lee.

Somewhat like his analysis of the United States Constitution, he argued that the Bible did not offer a clear description regarding who should be enslaved. Lacking this, the whole practice of bondage depended on raw power to claim ownership of other people. Lee granted that Scripture referred to slavery, but this did not mean the Bible sanctioned such abuse. In fact, Lee understood the sacred text as a divine judgment on worldly power. He reasoned that "the texts relied upon to support slavery, do not prove that it ever

37. Lee, *Slavery Examined*, 1.
38. Capers, *Southern Christian Advocate*, 150.
39. Parker, *Letter to the People*, 75.
40. Lee, *Slavery Examined*, 29.

existed in the Church, and that, if it did exist, they do not prove it is right."[41] Lee insisted that the ordering of human relationships must move beyond the way things are toward the way things ought to be.

In the spring of 1855 Lee was summoned to become pastor of the Wesleyan Church in Fulton, New York—the location of his earlier service as a Methodist Episcopal pastor. During the three years in Syracuse and the first several months in Fulton, Lee wrote his *Elements of Theology*. He later recalled that when the manuscript was completed there were no funds to publish the book. A generous member of the Fulton church stepped forward and provided $1,000 for the effort.[42]

Lee presumed that his pastorate in Fulton would be a long one, but events unfolded that made the stay shorter than anticipated. In early 1856 he was approached by an agent from Leoni College in Michigan. The school at Leoni had been founded in the middle 1840s and was situated near Jackson, Michigan (some eighty miles west of Detroit). Officials from the college wanted Lee to join their faculty, and his *Elements of Theology* offered a standard for educating Wesleyan Methodist clergy. By the summer of 1856, Luther and Mary Lee were settling into their new Michigan home.

Lee's text on theology ran to some 577 pages. It addressed traditional doctrines—from a Wesleyan perspective: the existence and attributes of God, the authority of the Scriptures, the order of salvation, and the ministry of Christ's church. It also emphasized "God's moral government," the organization of humanity according to divine law.[43] For such a lengthy and academic treatment, Lee did bring his perspective home with rather pithy claims. When considering human legislation, he bluntly stated, "Law is based upon right, not right upon law."[44] This was consistent with his earlier sermons and speeches regarding the higher law, but here it was placed within an overall theological context.

Among the consideration of God's law, Lee introduced a philosophical framework that attempted to define human nature. Accordingly, people were understood to have three distinct attributes: intelligence, sensibility (or feelings), and free will. This threefold formula was not unique to Lee. Many of his era embraced a similar "faculty psychology"—a formal description of

41. Lee, *Slavery Examined*, 184.

42. Lee, *Autobiography*, 290–91.

43. Lee, *Elements of Theology*, 332.

44. Lee, *Elements of Theology*, 334.

human personality. Abolitionist philosopher Asa Mahan had written a book on the subject in 1845, and Lee referenced Mahan's treatment.[45]

As Lee saw things, the obligation to obey divine law required rightly ordered mental faculties. The intellect must perceive clearly, and the sensibilities must not lead one into selfishness. Most especially, the free will must choose and act upon that which is right. The proper coordination of these faculties became critical to other abolitionists. Sojourner Truth's friend Gilbert Haven made it the topic of his college graduation address.[46] Later Haven invoked the three faculties when preaching about God's higher law.[47]

The college in Leoni promised to be a rich environment for Luther Lee's teaching and writing, but by the fall of 1857 financial troubles plagued the school. Lee accepted a parish appointment in southern Ohio, staying for two years and then took a position in Chagrin Falls, near Cleveland. While serving in Chagrin Falls, Lee responded to another abolitionist crisis of national proportions.

On October 16, 1859, John Brown (1800–1859) and a small "army" assaulted the federal arsenal at Harpers Ferry, Virginia (now West Virginia). They hoped to start an uprising that would free enslaved people. However, their plan fell to pieces when they found themselves pinned down. Finally, a contingent of United States marines attacked, killing many of the twenty-two raiders and wounding Brown. John Brown was tried for treason and convicted. He was hanged on December 2, 1859.

Historians are still divided over the stability and purposes of Brown. Was he a freedom fighter or a disturbed criminal? Most Americans recoiled in horror at Brown's actions. Yet many abolitionists considered him a hero. Luther Lee was one such defender.

John Brown had spent his early years in Hudson, Ohio—fifteen miles from Chagrin Falls. Sometime in early 1860 Lee preached a sermon in the Congregational Church of Chagrin Falls with the title "Dying to the Glory of God." The address revolved around one claim: In resisting slavery and dying for the cause, Brown honored God. For Luther Lee and many others, he was a legitimate martyr. To those who abhorred Brown's violation of the civil law, Lee quoted John Wesley: "Notwithstanding ten thousand laws, right is right, and wrong is wrong."[48] There was certainly an apocalyptic quality to events

45. Lee, *Elements of Theology*, 186, 336; Mahan, *Doctrine of the Will.*

46. Haven, "Philosophical Oration," 1.

47. Haven, *National Sermons*, 1–32.

48. Lee, *Five Sermons and a Tract*, 109. See also, Wesley, "Thoughts upon Slavery," 70.

in Harpers Ferry, but through his boldness, Brown sounded the death knell for human bondage in America.

This unapologetic eulogy for John Brown declared how far Lee was prepared to go in his fight against slavery. Soon he received an invitation to preach a memorial sermon for Brown on July 4, 1860, at the grave of the executed abolitionist. Lee remembered, "I was called from my home in Ohio to deliver an oration from the rock overhanging John Brown's grave. That was the oration of my life, the most radical and, probably, the most able I ever delivered."[49] Brown was buried at his farm in North Elba, New York, among the Adirondack Mountains. His widow issued the invitation for Lee to speak.

It was no accident that the tribute to Brown happened on July 4. Some twelve hundred people descended on the family's farm to claim a sacred link between the patriots of America's revolution and their Harpers Ferry martyr. The pastor who introduced Lee described him as "a man who believes in the Bible, and the Declaration of Independence; in Bunker Hill, and Harper's Ferry."[50] Lee did not disappoint and insisted that enslaved people had a right to rise up and take their liberty: "This was the foundation principle of the Revolution, and is emphatically the American idea."[51] As for John Brown, Lee admitted, "He may have erred in regard to time and manner and circumstances, but the principle involved I defend, upon the grounds of the Declaration of American Independence."[52] Such dramatic preaching was not without detractors, but it left an unmistakable impression.

Less than a year after Lee's sermon, America was at war with itself over slavery. During the winter and spring of 1864, he was invited to become a professor of theology at Adrian College in Michigan. The Adrian school had been chartered in 1859 as a successor to the faltering institute at Leoni. Following the Civil War, he rejoined the Methodist Episcopal Church and died in December of 1889. He is buried in Glenwood Cemetery, Flint, Michigan.

49. Lee, *Autobiography*, 295.

50. Quoted in Kaufman, *"Logical" Luther Lee*, 190.

51. Lee, "Fourth of July Oration," 121.

52. Lee, "Fourth of July Oration," 122.

**Faces carved into the basement wall of the Wesleyan Methodist Church
in Syracuse, New York may be the artwork of people leaving slavery on
the Underground Railroad.**

Image Courtesy of the Onondaga Historical Association,
Syracuse, New York

Over the years, the Wesleyan Methodist Church building on the
corner of Onondaga and Jefferson Streets in Syracuse has served many
purposes. Most notably, it became the site of a popular restaurant. The
church, of course, is not the building but the people. However, this building was destined to offer hospitality. It has radiated welcome in contemporary times—and more poignantly served as a haven for those seeking
freedom on the Underground Railroad. Luther Lee hosted hundreds
of people leaving slavery while in Syracuse. He also wrote exceedingly
detailed work in theology there. For him, theory and practice belonged
together. Perhaps that is his greatest legacy.

Chapter IV

LAURA HAVILAND

Between the Lids of the Bible

A Fathomless Fountain

On Thursday afternoon, June 24, 1909, in Adrian, Michigan, a granite drinking fountain was dedicated for public use. This was no ordinary civic improvement. The "memorial fountain" stood on a massive base and featured a statue of nineteenth century reformer Laura Smith Haviland.

Haviland (1808–98) had been a legendary educator, public health advocate, and temperance leader throughout Michigan, Ohio, and other regions. The memorial in Adrian was paid for by citizen contributions and by primary sponsorship of the Women's Christian Temperance Union. Founded in 1874, the WCTU fought alcoholism, and elaborate public drinking fountains became a trademark of the organization. They met a practical social need—while offering a healthy alternative to alcoholic beverages. It made sense that Laura Haviland would be honored in such a signature way, but there was an even deeper meaning to her memorial.[1]

The dedicatory plaque attached to the statue quoted Matt 25:35: "I was thirsty and ye gave me drink." What could be more appropriate for a monument extolling the virtues of pure water?

However, today Haviland is perhaps best remembered for her work on the Underground Railroad. Before the Civil War she and her family offered food, drink, and lodging to scores of people leaving slavery. The Haviland

---

1. "Aunt Laura Haviland Memorial Fountain," 7.

farm, located in rural Lenawee County, Michigan, served as a refuge for many who had few friends. After all, the teaching from Matt 25 is about radical hospitality more than anything else. We are to see Jesus in vulnerable people. In fact, that is one way we meet him today. Jesus did not focus on pure drinking water; he raised engagement with others to a divine level. Laura Haviland got the point and, more importantly, lived this imperative when she hosted those heading to Canada on the Underground Railroad.

Laura Smith (Haviland) was born in Ontario on December 20, 1808, and came of age among a devout Quaker family. The Quakers (or members of the Religious Society of Friends) were simple and thoughtful people. As a child, young Laura seemed a sensitive soul. Later she remembered asking incessant questions of her parents about the world, about God, about human relationships, about reality itself.

One starry night she looked up and saw the heavens so evenly arrayed around her home. It seemed as if she stood at the center of the universe. When she traveled with family some miles to visit her grandparents, she conducted an experiment. Smith gazed at the stars from that vantage point, just as she had in her own yard. She anticipated seeing the heavens arranged a bit differently from this new location, but they were spread out just as they had been at her home. Her grandparents lived at the center of the universe, too! How could this be? No matter where she traveled, she found herself at the center of the universe.

Later she observed the way "grown-up children are prone to think their own nation is ahead in arts and sciences, of all other nations—their own State ahead of all other States in moral and intellectual improvements—their own town or city, like Boston, the 'hub of the universe.'"[2] She never invoked this experience to argue for moral relativism, but she did insist that the self be dethroned in order to worship God.

Soon Smith encountered slavery and its effects. Her family moved to New York State and settled in Lockport, a town "that grew up as by magic upon the Erie Canal."[3] She hungered for knowledge and read every book within reach. The writings of New Jersey Quaker John Woolman made a lasting impression—especially his indictment of human bondage, and she witnessed the abuse suffered by African Americans in her own village. At the same time her inquisitive mind drank deeply from the well of spiritual

2. Haviland, *Woman's Life-Work* (1882), 11–12.
3. Haviland, *Woman's Life-Work* (1882), 14.

questions. Who was God? What was her place in God's creation? Would she live in eternity?

During the autumn of her thirteenth year, she received permission from her strict Quaker parents to attend a prayer meeting at an uncle's home. There she experienced singing, praying, and exuberant worship. It was a Methodist gathering. She resolved to process the dynamics of sin and grace and to confront her uncertainty about matters of faith. Young Smith was ridiculed by some for spending so much time with enthusiastic Methodists, but she persisted.

Her conflicted soul almost concluded that God was too good to damn anyone. Perhaps all people were ultimately saved. But she could not reconcile this possibility with the parable of Lazarus and the rich man, which emphasized accountability (Luke 16:19–31). At other times she considered that perhaps only an elect few were saved and that she was among the hopeless. In a state of near despair, she attended more prayer meetings.

One day, while walking to her grandfather's home, she considered humanity and her own condition: "Is there no balm in Gilead? is there no physician there to heal this sin-stricken world, this sin-sick soul of mine?"[4] The answer struck her as a terrible and wonderful gift: "Yes, Jesus is that balm; he shed his own precious blood for me on Calvary, that I might live now, and for evermore!"[5] She bore the responsibility for receiving or rejecting this gift, and she pondered its implications for humanity. As a youth she had nurtured prejudice against many who were not like her. Now she saw that each and all were, alike, loved by a God who went to the cross. Later she called this love "a fathomless fountain," and it grounded her entire approach to human rights.[6]

When she was sixteen, Laura Smith met a young man named Charles Haviland, Jr., and they were married on November 3, 1825, in Lockport. During September of 1829, the couple moved to Lenawee County, Michigan Territory. Many of their family members also lived in that region, and Laura Haviland experienced a series of spiritual highs and lows as she settled into the Michigan wilderness. In 1832 she helped organize an antislavery society with her neighbor, Elizabeth Margaret Chandler (1807–34).

Chandler was, likewise, a member of the Religious Society of Friends—born in Delaware and educated in Philadelphia. She displayed

4. Haviland, *Woman's Life-Work* (1882), 19.
5. Haviland, *Woman's Life-Work* (1882), 19–20.
6. Haviland, *Woman's Life-Work* (1882), 20.

gifts as a poet and died from disease before her posthumous writing received critical praise. Haviland lost a kindred soul but soldiered on as a determined abolitionist.

In 1837 Charles and Laura Haviland, along with her brother Harvey Smith, opened a manual labor school. The family hosted nine children from the surrounding area who struggled in poverty, in addition to their own four children. Together they pursued a course of vocational arts and academic foundations. However, this enterprise did not receive the financial support required, and the fledgling school was closed. Soon a new venture came alive.[7]

The Havilands and Harvey Smith were inspired by the Oberlin Collegiate Institute (now Oberlin College), which had received African American students in 1835. The three redoubled their efforts and opened the Raisin Institute in 1839. It became the first integrated school in Michigan and sat on family property in rural Raisin Township, Lenawee County. Perched above the gentle slopes of the River Raisin Valley, the institute provided bucolic protection for learning. The Haviland home, the school, and the farm were a haven for youngsters, and soon it became known as a stop on the Underground Railroad.

While many Quakers distinguished themselves among the antislavery cause, those nearest to Laura Haviland thought such advocacy too controversial. This created an unbearable tension for her, and she resolved to leave the Quaker fold. The year 1839 not only marked the birth of the Raisin Institute; it also became the year Haviland and many of her extended family withdrew from the Religious Society of Friends.[8]

The dynamics surrounding this exodus are instructive, and the letter of withdrawal reads,

> We, the undersigned, do say there is a diversity of sentiment existing in the Society on the divine authority of the Holy Scriptures, the resurrection of the dead, and day of judgment, justification by faith, the effect of Adam's fall upon his posterity, and the abolition of slavery, which has caused a disunity amongst us; and there being no hope of a reconciliation by investigation, ministers being told by ruling members that there is to be no other test of the soundness of their ministry but something in their own breasts, thus virtually denying the Holy Scriptures to be the test of doctrine;—we, therefore, do wish quietly to withdraw from the

7. Haviland, *Woman's Life-Work* (1882), 34.
8. Mull, *Underground Railroad*, 42.

Monthly Meeting, and thus resign our right of membership with the Society of Friends.[9]

According to Haviland, the letter was signed by twenty people.

The separation named differences over slavery, but there were also several doctrinal matters of contention. Among other points, those leaving the Friends stressed the authority of Scripture. This did not mean that the Bible was unimportant in Quaker communities, but here there appeared to be irreconcilable differences regarding the source of moral principles. Should one rely on the Scriptures or personal conscience? The two were not mutually exclusive, but Haviland and her family emphasized the former, while many established Quakers stressed the latter.

The withdrawal did not go unchallenged. Joseph John Gurney (1788–1847), the well-known English Quaker, wrote a specific rebuttal to Haviland and her compatriots. According to him, it was not true that the Religious Society of Friends undervalued Scripture and neglected the other doctrines at issue. However, his defense drew from appeals to "the light of Christ" and "conscience."[10] He also declared that Quakers "have always upheld the influence of the Holy Spirit operating immediately on the mind of man, as the *primary source* of all true knowledge of the things of God."[11] Laura Haviland revered the role of the Holy Spirit, but she also knew that claiming the Spirit's direction, apart from Scripture, can lead to antinomianism.

Haviland's dispute with her ancestral community of faith is typically overlooked or downplayed in popular treatments of her life. Even the memorial fountain in Adrian portrays her as the quintessential Quaker woman— complete with traditional bonnet. Yet from 1839 until 1872 she lived and worked in self-imposed exile from the Religious Society of Friends.

The journey out of her established tradition did invite a question. What Christian community would sustain her going forward? As matters unfolded, Haviland and many of those who left the Friends joined the new Wesleyan Methodist Connection—a movement that was developing in Michigan even before Luther Lee and others farther east established the denomination. Haviland's affiliation with the Wesleyan Methodists was intimately related to that body's witness against slavery. But her fit with the Wesleyans also revolved around theological emphases—the authority

9. Haviland, *Woman's Life-Work* (1882), 33.

10. Gurney, *Letter to Friends of the Monthly Meeting*, 5, 11.

11. Gurney, *Letter to Friends of the Monthly Meeting*, 10.

of Scripture, salvation by grace through faith, and the core Wesleyan belief that Christ's atoning death was for every human being.

Throughout her life Haviland nurtured a fascination with and respect for the meaning of dreams. For her, these nocturnal experiences were not simply psychological fantasies. She believed that they revealed deeper truths. Sometime in the early 1840s Haviland dreamed that she was standing in her front yard, with family, when an angel riding a bay horse descended and said, "Follow thou me." Haviland responded to the angel that she would follow as soon as she said goodbye to her family. The angel insisted, "Let the dead bury their dead, but follow thou me." She followed the angel to a graveyard, where he left her. Then she awoke.[12]

The unsettling dream haunted her, but later she concluded that it was sent to prepare her for pending tragedy. During the late winter and early spring of 1845, an epidemic swept through the community. The disease, erysipelas, was caused by a bacterial infection and in Haviland's day often proved fatal. Her husband was struck down and died on March 13, 1845. Soon her mother, father, and twenty-two-month-old daughter died. Haviland became dangerously ill but recovered.

She remembered, "It seemed that my last earthly prop was gone."[13] Barely strong enough for ordinary tasks, she attempted to care for remaining family and their small farm. She discovered a crushing debt attached to her land and anticipated that the fall harvest would cover but one-half of the obligation. Haviland contacted her creditors and explained her situation, noting that she was now left alone with seven minor children. The creditors were not much help, and one openly scoffed at her for attempting to continue the family's farming business.

In the face of obstacles that would destroy most people, she took her case to "the widow's God."[14] Then she had another dream. An angelic host appeared to her. One of the beings took Haviland's hand, and she felt confident enough to ask for a name. "My name is Supporter," the angel replied. Haviland asked about another figure and received an answer: "Her name is Influencer-of-hearts." A third angel was named "Searcher-of-hearts." Haviland realized that the names of each angel revealed a divine mission.[15]

12. Haviland, *Woman's Life-Work* (1882), 38.
13. Haviland, *Woman's Life-Work* (1882), 46.
14. Haviland, *Woman's Life-Work* (1882), 48.
15. Haviland, *Woman's Life-Work* (1882), 48–49.

One of the beings said to Supporter, "Support her, for she needs it." The angel by that named reached for Haviland's other hand. With both of her hands in the comforting grasp of this guardian, a wave of strength passed over her and filled her soul. She was not alone. Her troubles remained, but she woke with a sense of peace: "Calm and sweet was this confidence in being cared for, and supported by an almighty arm."[16] Not even crushing grief and insensitivity could keep her down.

A few days after the dream, one of her inflexible creditors called, saying he would not demand payment that fall. The news arrived as a most profound grace. Haviland thanked the man but reserved her deepest praise for the Lord of all. This was no easy triumph, but it was a victory, nonetheless.

It is impossible to understand Laura Haviland apart from her searing confrontation with loss and grief. These forces presented unimaginable trauma that threatened to break her and isolate her from others. She never attempted to minimize the pain, and she also never surrendered to its toxic hold. God transformed her, whether through or despite the experience one cannot say. The brutality of it all escapes easy explanation. When the dust finally settled, Haviland was bent, beaten, and bruised by life but not completely broken, and she emerged stronger than ever—empowered to serve Jesus in astounding ways.

Principles of Equal Rights

Haviland's experiences were immortalized in a book, first published during 1881. *A Woman's Life-Work* ran to more than five hundred pages and is best remembered for its riveting tales about work on the Underground Railroad. She excelled at this kind of storytelling, and though written years after most events, we have no reason to suspect the general integrity of her recollection.

One of the first episodes shared by Haviland focused on the lives of Willis and Elsie Hamilton. Willis Hamilton was enslaved in Tennessee and became free. He then sought the liberation of his wife from a neighboring plantation. Together they journeyed to Michigan and were welcomed by the Havilands. The couple farmed in several northern locations as they sought the whereabouts of their two daughters, still living in slavery.

The Hamiltons sent a letter to an individual in Tennessee known as Deacon Bayliss. This man had freed Willis after a conviction of conscience,

16. Haviland, *Woman's Life-Work* (1882), 48–49.

and perhaps he could help find their daughters. Soon they received a response from someone purporting to be Deacon Bayliss, and through a series of correspondence, the Hamiltons were told that their old acquaintance was on business in northern Ohio. They were asked to meet him at a hotel in Toledo, less than fifty miles away.

The Hamiltons and Haviland were wary. Was this a plot to take Elsie back into slavery and to deny Willis his freedom? Haviland, her son Daniel, and a friend named James Martin rode the train to Toledo and discovered that the man purporting to be Bayliss was in fact an abusive Tennessee plantation owner named John P. Chester. Chester claimed to "own" Elsie Hamilton.

The conniving Tennessean was not alone but surrounded by henchmen, including his son, ready to abduct the Hamiltons. Over the course of a lengthy confrontation, the would-be abductors tried to plead innocence, but Haviland was having none of it. She saw through their plot and called them out. For her trouble, she and her traveling companions were threatened at gun point. Eventually, bitter southerners placed a $3,000 bounty on her.

Often missed in such stories are those moments when Haviland expressed the rationale and resolve for her action. For instance, in Toledo, she delivered a scathing articulation regarding why slavery is wrong: It contravenes "the laws of eternal right given by God."[17] She continued, "I firmly believe in our Declaration of Independence, that all men are created free and equal, and that no human being has a right to make merchandise of others born in humbler stations."[18] It is true that such statements were woven throughout her narrative after the fact, but they also appear to have motivated her when she acted. The fact that they are featured in her book demonstrates their lasting significance.

In the autumn of 1847, a suspicious character visited the Haviland farm, claiming to be an Ohio schoolteacher. For an educator, he asked an unusual number of questions about the Underground Railroad and the location of some who had escaped slavery. Was he another trickster seeking to abduct someone? Haviland identified his ploy and told the man that anyone trying to seize people in her region would face determined resistance from the public. The visitor insisted, with mock innocence, that

17. Haviland, *Woman's Life-Work* (1882), 65.
18. Haviland, *Woman's Life-Work* (1882), 66.

LAURA HAVILAND

the citizenry could not stop such kidnapping because the law provided for the recapture of so-called fugitives.

At that Haviland retorted, "'I presume if the slave claimant should come with a score of witnesses and a half-bushel of papers, to prove his legal right, it would avail him nothing, as we claim a higher law than wicked enactments of men who claim the misnomer of law by which bodies and souls of men, women, and children are claimed as chattels.'"[19] Here she repeated a reference to "the wicked enactments of men" made earlier when defending Willis and Elsie Hamilton.[20] Such distorted human legislation was powerless when compared with the "higher law."

Some years later, Haviland solicited funds from Adrian, Michigan, business leaders to assist those leaving slavery. A recalcitrant banker scoffed at her request and proceeded to accuse her of spreading lies about slavery's severity. She confronted this man with the truth and eventually elicited a begrudging donation. She remembered, "Although it is unpleasant to meet with such spirits, yet I never flee from them. If my cause is owned by the author of the *Higher Law*, none of these things move me."[21] It is easy to overlook Haviland's explicit reliance on higher law thinking. She remains revered not so much for theoretical explication as for courageous living.

However, this does not mean that profound philosophical principles were absent from Haviland's work. Luther Lee wrote lengthy defenses of the higher law—and then lived it. Laura Haviland lived the higher law—and then explained why it was so important.

In 1849 the Raisin Institute closed for a period, due to financial struggles, but Haviland remained focused and continued her witness. She journeyed to Cincinnati on a mission to aid abolitionist Calvin Fairbank (1816–98). Fairbank was born in Pike, New York, and during 1837 began helping people on the Underground Railroad. He received ordination from the Methodist Episcopal Church in 1842 and desired further education. For a brief time, Fairbank attended the Oberlin Collegiate Institute. Soon he returned to helping those fleeing slavery, but by early 1845 he found himself serving prison time for his Underground Railroad activity.

Fairbank was released in August of 1849 and made his way to Cincinnati, where he discovered "old comrades in the holy work for humanity

19. Haviland, *Woman's Life-Work* (1882), 93.
20. Haviland, *Woman's Life-Work* (1882), 65.
21. Haviland, *Woman's Life-Work* (1882), 239.

81

against oppression."[22] There he met Laura Haviland for the first time. He spoke to antislavery gatherings and continued to advocate for freedom. Then following the Fugitive Slave legislation of 1850, he was asked to help an enslaved woman in Louisville, Kentucky. He crossed the Ohio River and returned to Indiana with her. Fairbank managed to send the woman on to safety, but he was arrested on November 9, 1851, and taken back to Louisville. As a repeat offender, he faced a bleak future.

Laura Haviland decided to visit Fairbank in the Louisville jail. She desired to give him warm clothing and other necessities. Most of Haviland's friends did not want her to enter the lion's den across the river, but she insisted.

The jailer in Louisville was a man known as Colonel Buckner, and Haviland noted that he was a Methodist class-leader. She intended to deliver her items of mercy and leave but was persuaded to stay a bit longer. During the visit, this jailer attempted to convince her that slavery was not all that evil and perhaps even benevolent. This argument did not go down well with Haviland, and she held her ground.

Finally, in exasperation, Colonel Buckner demanded to know where Haviland and other abolitionists found their principles of equal rights. To this, she gave an elaborate reply:

> We find them between the lids of the Bible. God created man in his own image—in his own likeness. From a single pair sprang all the inhabitants of the whole earth. God created of one blood all the nations that dwell upon the whole earth; and when the Savior left his abode with the Father, to dwell a season upon our earthly ball, to suffer and die the ignominious death of the cross, he shed his precious blood for the whole human family, irrespective of nation or color. We believe all are alike objects of redeeming love. We believe our Heavenly Father gave the power of choice to beings he created for his own glory; and this power to choose or refuse good or evil is a truth co-existent with man's creation. This, at least, is my firm conviction.[23]

Such an eloquent declaration summarized the motivating ideas for her entire life.

If this were Scripture, perhaps a letter written by the apostle Paul, scholars would speculate that the statement came from a separate fragment,

---

22. Fairbank, *Rev. Calvin Fairbank*, 60.
23. Haviland, *Woman's Life-Work* (1882), 149.

a short hymn, or a poem. It may have been inserted to reinforce a fundamental point. One thinks of the lyrical text found in Phil 2 or some other distinct passage. Haviland's declaration stands as a recapitulation of principles for abolitionists and reads like a creed—complete with "we believe" language. Moreover, it is presented as a distillation of biblical truth.

During an era when many were quoting Scripture to refute modern human rights, Haviland did the opposite. Her appeal to the Bible buttressed notions of equality, sacredness, and philosophically grounded action. Years earlier Haviland cited her reverence for "the divine authority of the Holy Scriptures" as one reason for separating from the Quakers.[24] She firmly believed in accountability to the Bible and concluded that this required a respect for rights.

A parsing of Haviland's declaration bears much fruit. She opened by referencing the idea that humanity was created in God's image (Gen 1:26). She did not elaborate on this conviction but stated it in a way to underscore the dignity and worth of people—all people. Then she declared that "God created of one blood all the nations that dwell upon the whole earth."[25] This terminology, from Acts 17:26, appears more than once throughout her autobiography.

When confronting would-be abductors in Toledo, Haviland embraced "the laws of eternal right given by God, who made of one blood all nations who dwell upon the face of the earth."[26] During the Civil War she spoke to a community of recently freed people in Tennessee, insisting that God "made all the nations of the whole earth of one blood, and never designed that one race should hold another in bondage."[27] Following the war, she met a Confederate general in Virginia who proceeded to accuse abolitionists of stealing southern "property." Haviland shot back, "God never designed that we should make merchandise of human beings. In the written Word we find that God made of one blood all the nations of the earth."[28] An 1887 edition of her narrative quotes Acts 17:26 on the very last page.[29]

Haviland was not alone in emphasizing this text from Acts. Several others made language regarding "one blood" a signature of their antislavery

24. Haviland, *Woman's Life-Work* (1882), 33.

25. Haviland, *Woman's Life-Work* (1882), 149.

26. Haviland, *Woman's Life-Work* (1882), 65.

27. Haviland, *Woman's Life-Work* (1882), 266.

28. Haviland, *Woman's Life-Work* (1882), 420.

29. Haviland, *Woman's Life-Work* (1887), 554.

argument. Luther Lee welded the principles found in the Declaration of Independence with the teaching from Acts 17:26.[30]

On July 5, 1827, Nathaniel Paul, pastor of the First African Baptist Society in Albany, New York, celebrated the abolition of slavery in that state with a memorable address. Paul invoked the "God who has made of one blood all nations" to condemn the crime of human bondage.[31] He predicted that slavery would be abolished throughout the world.

These references to humanity's created attributes of dignity and common value served an important function. They coincided with the philosophies of natural rights that were gaining ground after the American Revolution. Yet, as a Christian, Haviland also rooted her advocacy in the redeemed value of people conferred by the life, death, and resurrection of Jesus. She declared to the Louisville jailer that Christ "shed his precious blood for the whole human family, irrespective of nation or color."[32] Human beings certainly possessed a created worth, but her faith also taught that the atonement offered a reaffirmation of value. People are doubly sacred.

Haviland encountered the redeemed worth of others early in her life. She was awestruck by the notion that "Jesus shed his blood to redeem all who would by faith accept salvation so freely offered."[33] During childhood, this truth compelled her to respect people of African descent and Native Americans. As an adult such expansive love motivated her work to end slavery. The Tennessee camp of freed people who heard her emphasize the "one blood" of humanity was also told that "our Lord and Savior died upon the cross for all alike, because he is no respecter of persons."[34] After the Civil War, she pledged that Southerners would "never again barter for paltry gold the bodies and souls of those whom Christ died to redeem with his own precious blood."[35] The sacrifice of Jesus gave new life to human dignity.

Haviland's dependence on the atonement to underwrite her witness may seem clichéd or perfunctory. It was not. Followers of John Wesley, in contrast to some Christians, taught that Jesus died for every human being. Others taught a more limited atonement. When Haviland looked the Louisville jailer in the eyes and challenged slavery, she was wielding Wesleyan

---

30. Lee, *Slavery Examined*, 29.

31. Paul, *Address, Delivered on the Celebration of the Abolition of Slavery*, 15.

32. Haviland, *Woman's Life-Work* (1882), 149.

33. Haviland, *Woman's Life-Work* (1882), 20.

34. Haviland, *Woman's Life-Work* (1882), 265.

35. Haviland, *Woman's Life-Work* (1882), 414.

theology against him. How could he claim to be a genuine Methodist class-leader when he supported such a heinous institution?

The theology of atonement embraced by Haviland also required that people have some measure of free will. Every single person on earth was valued by a God who went to the cross, but each person bore responsibility to receive or reject this love. Additionally, there were profound moral issues at stake. Free will accompanied the personal dynamics of redemption, but it stood at the center of righteous living, too. The will expressed a "power to choose or refuse good or evil" itself.[36] Luther Lee had emphasized the three faculties of the human mind (intellect, sensibility, and free will), and Laura Haviland saw her witness through the same prism.

Not long after working in Cincinnati and Louisville, Haviland became acquainted with Henry Bibb (1815–54). Bibb was born an enslaved person in Shelby County, Kentucky. Following several escape attempts, he finally freed himself and arrived in Detroit during January of 1842. He sought an education, with the help of an abolitionist pastor, and eventually moved to Sandwich, Canada West (now Windsor, Ontario).

Bibb and his wife Mary helped organize the Refugee Home Society near Sandwich in 1851. Soon Haviland was approached by Henry Bibb, Horace Hallack, and Charles C. Foote. They invited her to teach among this colony of recently liberated people. As Haviland remembered, "The settlers had built for themselves small log-houses, and cleared from one to five acres each on their heavily timbered land, and raised corn, potatoes, and other garden vegetables."[37] During the autumn of 1852, she opened a school among the community.

The school was designed "for every body of any age," and it was filled to capacity.[38] Haviland recalled that many people came from five or six miles away each Sunday. Those who could read passages of Scripture did so, and lively conversation followed. Others brought legal documents so that Haviland might clarify any uncertainties. More than once, she helped newcomers avoid being cheated by slick opportunists. Her time in Canada offered a change of scenery and lasting friendship, but Lenawee County remained her home. When she returned to Michigan, she spent several years preparing to reopen the Raisin Institute.

36. Haviland, *Woman's Life-Work* (1882), 149.

37. Haviland, *Woman's Life-Work* (1882), 192.

38. Haviland, *Woman's Life-Work* (1882), 192.

This Confusion of Our Nation's Shame

On August 10, 1860, the front page of the *Adrian Daily Expositor* featured a letter written by Laura Haviland. The missive, dated July 4, 1860, told a harrowing tale of escape from slavery and reunion. Not two weeks before, six people presented themselves at Haviland's door. One of the travelers was a young man bearing a sad countenance. He and his wife were separated, and the closer he got to Canada, the more he despaired of finding her. She had been able to free herself and journey north; he was delayed in making his escape. Now he sought her with determination and fading hope.

Haviland inquired after the woman's name and realized that she was living a mere fifteen miles away. The news so thrilled the man that joy "seemed to electrify his entire being."[39] His wife was Mary Todd, and she was staying at the home of Fitch and Ann Reed in Cambridge Township, Lenawee County.[40]

Fitch Reed (1814–97) was a farmer who served as a faithful host on the Underground Railroad. He became a steadfast leader within the Wesleyan Methodist movement and sat on the board of trustees at nearby Adrian College. This college had been founded in 1859 by Wesleyan Methodists, and their first president was Asa Mahan, the acclaimed educator from the Oberlin Collegiate Institute. Mahan owned a well-earned reputation for Wesleyan thinking and abolitionist conviction, making him a natural for the post. During the summer of 1860 the new college was in the middle of a building campaign.

The first annual commencement of Adrian College took place on Tuesday, June 12, 1860. It was a commencement in name only. No degrees were granted. Yet the occasion offered an opportunity to place a cornerstone for the campus chapel. Speeches were given, and dignitaries graced the celebration. The keynote guest for the event was none other than Luther Lee, then living in Chagrin Falls, Ohio. Lee claimed that the purpose of education was to give "more ample scope to our mental faculties."[41] Like Asa Mahan, he believed that the proper ordering of the mind led to righteous action. Lee's address featured typical platitudes about the improvement of humanity, but soon he would engage in more

---

39. Haviland, "Story of Slavery and Deliverance," 1.

40. Haviland, *Woman's Life-Work* (1882), 213.

41. "First Annual Commencement," 1.

controversial advocacy. Within a month Lee was holding forth in North Elba, New York, at the grave of John Brown.

Laura Haviland wrote her story for the *Adrian Daily Expositor* on the very same day that Lee eulogized Brown in New York. Like Lee, she contrasted the meaning of July 4 with the contemptible existence of slavery. Haviland was not satisfied to narrate the tale of Mary Todd and her husband. She framed the story within a commentary about American principles. The lead sentence read, "The cannon's roar and beating drum of to-day cannot annihilate the bitter groans, or fast falling tears of the southern slave."[42] Fourth of July celebrations demanded brutal honesty. Those declaring that people possess "inalienable rights, to life, liberty, and the pursuit of happiness" could not ignore the band of travelers at her door.[43]

Haviland termed the hypocrisy of lauding freedom and holding others in slavery "this confusion of our nation's shame."[44] She leveled such blistering critique because she loved her country, not because she sought its condemnation. Within a year, America erupted into Civil War, and seventeen students from the Raisin Institute enlisted in the Union forces. Haviland kept the school going during the war's early years, but by the spring of 1864 matters became untenable.[45]

The longer the war lasted, the more Haviland felt a tug toward charitable work among wounded soldiers. In 1863 she left a preceptress in charge of the Institute and made her way to Chicago. Bearing fifteen dollars and several boxes of supplies, she sought a free railroad pass to Cairo, Illinois, at the confluence of the Mississippi and Ohio Rivers.[46]

By that point in the war Cairo was a sprawling supply depot for the Union cause, featuring mud, wharf rats, and every conceivable vice. Haviland waded right in and visited hospitals brimming with soldiers. There were camps full of recently freed people, too, and the army proposed to move many of them down river to a place known as Island Number Ten—a small outpost in the Mississippi. This island was located near the Kentucky-Tennessee border and across the river from New Madrid, Missouri. Early in the war it had been taken from Confederate forces by Union gunboats.

42. Haviland, "Story of Slavery and Deliverance," 1.
43. Haviland, "Story of Slavery and Deliverance," 1.
44. Haviland, "Story of Slavery and Deliverance," 1.
45. Haviland, *Woman's Life-Work* (1882), 241–42.
46. Haviland, *Woman's Life-Work* (1882), 241–42.

When Haviland arrived on the island, she found two hundred and fifty acres of plow land with an orchard. Seven hundred freed people were already tilling the soil and tending the trees. There were signs of heavy bombardment everywhere: solid shot and shell littered the fields. Haviland went to work delivering clothing to those in need.[47]

An officer approached Haviland with happy tears: "Have you ever thought of the Savior's words, 'Inasmuch as ye have done it unto the *least* of these, ye have done it unto me?'"[48] Haviland responded, "That thought had come to my mind before engaging in this mission, and it is that which drew me from my Michigan home."[49] Long before words from Matt 25 were etched on the plaque of a memorial drinking fountain in Adrian, they animated her interaction with others.

The summer of 1863 brought the Battle of Gettysburg and the fall of Vicksburg, Mississippi. The Raisin Institute opened for the academic year 1863–1864 on Wednesday, September 2. Though enrollment was dwindling, Haviland believed the operation sound enough for more visits south. She secured a traveling companion by the name of Letitia Backus (1817–86). Letitia and Anson Backus were stalwart Wesleyan Methodists from west of Adrian. Their daughter, Mary (1843–1905), became the first female graduate of Adrian College in 1863. Haviland and her friends were more than one-dimensional abolitionists They also nurtured a legacy of women's rights advocacy.[50]

Haviland, now with Backus along, returned to Cairo, Illinois, and visited more hospitals. They waited for supplies to catch up with them and then headed down river to Columbus, Kentucky. As they toured hospitals the pair demanded better care for the wounded. Military authorities, hospital administrators, doctors, and nurses all came in for the same stern correction. Several times the two were able to improve conditions. It was a fearsome thing to be on the receiving end of a Haviland-Backus critique.[51]

At one hospital, they found several patients passing the time with a deck of cards. Haviland produced "an armful of Testaments" and suggested a trade: She would take the cards and leave the Bibles for the young men.

47. Haviland, *Woman's Life-Work* (1882), 250.

48. Haviland, *Woman's Life-Work* (1882), 253.

49. Haviland, *Woman's Life-Work* (1882), 253.

50. Haviland, *Woman's Life-Work* (1882), 279.

51. Haviland, *Woman's Life-Work* (1882), 279–81.

No one challenged her proposal.[52] The two women were not uncomfortable deploying motherly concern, but they did so with a toughness that won considerable respect. Before long they were on their way again down the Mississippi, headed for Vicksburg.

Near Napoleon, Arkansas, their boat was threatened by Confederate guerrillas. This irregular band plotted to capture the vessel while it stopped to take on wood. The boat shoved off in a hurry, and it was a close call. While the craft struggled to escape, a Union officer inquired about Haviland's well-being. She replied, "The God of Daniel lives at this hour."[53] References to the biblical Daniel's trust in a mighty God appear throughout her autobiography.[54]

Haviland and Backus reached Vicksburg but were summoned further along, to Natchez, where there was much suffering. The two set up shop near a camp of four thousand freed people who were living in deplorable conditions. While working there, Union and Confederate forces clashed not two miles distant. Many of the Union soldiers were African American, and this was soon after Confederates gave no quarter to black troops at Fort Pillow, Tennessee. A Union officer told Haviland that his men fought so fiercely their conduct bordered on vengeance. Haviland never subscribed to retribution as an acceptable military motive, but she did understand the soldiers' rage.[55]

The Michigan pair then crossed the Mississippi and took aid to people near Vidalia, Louisiana. There Haviland acquired an iron collar and a knee-stiffener—devices used by sadistic plantation owners to torture enslaved people. She vowed to take the relics north so those who denied slavery's evil would be confronted with chilling evidence.[56]

---

52. Haviland, *Woman's Life-Work* (1882), 281.
53. Haviland, *Woman's Life-Work* (1882), 284.
54. Haviland, *Woman's Life-Work* (1882), 156, 216, 284, 437, and 449.
55. Haviland, *Woman's Life-Work* (1882), 285.
56. Haviland, *Woman's Life-Work* (1882), 292–93.

During the Civil War, Laura Haviland (1808–1898) visited southern plantations
and collected evidence of the torture endured by enslaved people.

Image Courtesy of the National Portrait Gallery,
Smithsonian Institution

At New Orleans Haviland and Backus stopped by schools for freed
people and distributed more aid. Then they were asked to visit Ship Island
in the Gulf of Mexico. Ship Island was a small speck off the coast of Mississippi, almost seventy miles from New Orleans. In those days it was eight
miles long and less than a mile wide. The islet had been seized by Union
forces in 1861, and during the war it held both Union soldiers convicted of
crimes and Confederate prisoners of war.[57]

57. Haviland, *Woman's Life-Work* (1882), 320–25.

While on the island Haviland and Backus were hosted by the family of a Union army officer named Noyce. As they got to know their new friends, Backus spotted a book on a nearby table. The volume looked familiar. It was *The Life of Rev. Orange Scott*, written by Lucius Matlack. Among that forsaken piece of sand, Haviland and Backus encountered the biography of a legendary Wesleyan Methodist. But that was not all.

When Backus pointed to the book, their host lit up: "Do you know any thing of Orange Scott?"[58] Backus responded that she and Haviland knew all about Scott. After all, they were both Wesleyan Methodists. Their host beamed and revealed that she was, in fact, the daughter of Orange Scott! A reunion of spiritual kindred broke forth in the most unlikely place.

Haviland and Backus found that many of the Union prisoners on Ship Island were held under questionable charges—having been sentenced by a former Confederate officer who managed to secure for himself a post as judge advocate. The Michigan pair would not let this abuse of authority go unchallenged, and they went to work on behalf of the prisoners. Haviland wrote letters and met with senior military officials. She pursued the chain of command all the way up to the United States Congress, and eventually the prisoners were released. Hucksters, opportunists, and Confederate sympathizers were no match for Laura Haviland.[59]

In June of 1864 Haviland was appointed agent of a regional Freedmen's Aid Commission. She raised funds throughout Michigan and prepared "to return to the field of desolation."[60] The overwhelming task before her led to a painful decision. The Raisin Institute was closed so that she could devote her entire energy to relief work. By September 1864 Haviland had collected $400 and a load of supplies. This time she headed to Kansas.

At Leavenworth Haviland met J. R. Brown, John Brown's half-brother. Before his exploits at Harpers Ferry, John Brown participated in the violent struggle between proslavery forces from Missouri and Kansas abolitionists. Haviland's contact with the Brown family was not incidental. J. R. Brown helped her secure more resources and introduced her to those in need.[61]

She visited Lawrence, Kansas, and witnessed the aftermath of a heinous attack by Confederate guerrillas. Here William Quantrill and his partisans sacked the town in 1863. The indiscriminate killing of civilians and

58. Haviland, *Woman's Life-Work* (1882), 327.
59. Haviland, *Woman's Life-Work* (1882), 329–41.
60. Haviland, *Woman's Life-Work* (1882), 360.
61. Haviland, *Woman's Life-Work* (1882), 361.

the burning of buildings went down in history as a war crime. Haviland attended the local Methodist Episcopal Church, where seventy wounded, dying, and dead people had been brought in following the assault. There were still bloodstains on the church floor and some of the seats.[62]

As 1865 opened, Haviland found herself running low on supplies. She received a letter from the committee organizing a Ladies' State Freedmen's Fair in Detroit. Sponsors of the event wanted to display relics from slavery and the war. Haviland considered returning to Michigan for funds and materials. J. R. Brown suggested she take a Sharps rifle that had been used by his half-brother (John Brown) for exhibit at the fair. She did so willingly.[63]

Such moments in Haviland's life often go unnoticed, especially by those today who assume she was always a demure Quaker. She defied stereotypes, and her association with the Brown family invites serious questions. How did she view violence, even violence claiming to defend powerless people? There is no evidence that Haviland advocated vigilante justice, but she also avoided easy judgments against those fighting for freedom.

At the close of the Civil War in the spring of 1865, Haviland continued caring for destitute people. By August she was on her way to Washington, DC and beyond. She offered her resources and herself to all in need. At Fredericksburg, Virginia, and in Richmond, she did her best to help but met suspicion and resentment. It was during this time that Haviland found herself in the nation's capital, boarding that infamous streetcar with her friend Sojourner Truth.

Soon Haviland turned her attention toward establishing a public support system for homeless children. President Asa Mahan of Adrian College and his wife, Mary, joined the effort. Together, they and others petitioned the state of Michigan. Finally, in 1871, Michigan acted upon the proposal. The united resources of the public would pick up the challenge first accepted by Haviland. When the State Public School for orphans opened in Coldwater, Haviland moved there and worked for almost two years as a seamstress and nurse.[64]

In 1872 she returned to Adrian and became, once again, a member of the Religious Society of Friends. The reason for renewing her association with the Quakers was mentioned briefly in her autobiography. According to Haviland, "The spirit of missions became an increasing element in the

62. Haviland, *Woman's Life-Work* (1882), 369.
63. Haviland, *Woman's Life-Work* (1882), 373.
64. Haviland, *Woman's Life-Work* (1882), 477–81.

Society of Friends."[65] She made no reference to a change in theological conviction or dispute with the Wesleyans.

Haviland continued to serve people for the rest of her long life. She advocated for the well-being of freed people throughout the South and into western regions. In Kansas, a town was named after her. She died on April 20, 1898, and is buried in the Raisin Valley Friends Cemetery north of Adrian. When citizens erected her memorial in 1909, they had much to honor.

The Laura Haviland Memorial Fountain in Adrian, Michigan was dedicated on June 24, 1909.

Photo by Christopher P. Momany

65. Haviland, *Woman's Life-Work* (1882), 481.

A museum building stands next to Haviland's memorial fountain, and in its archives are a few small diaries kept by her during the 1890s. One entry notes a letter written to the daughter of Elsie and Willis Hamilton, the couple aided on the Underground Railroad years before.[66] Laura Haviland tended relationships up to the time of her death. The fathomless fountain of grace and the cup of cold water for others were one throughout her long life.

66. Haviland, "March 1, 1890."

Chapter V

HENRY BIBB

Voice of the Fugitive

The Inevitable Laws of Nature's God

ON A SUNNY MORNING in May of 2021, my wife, Elizabeth, and I drove slowly down a dirt road near Bedford, Kentucky. We parked in a field that began where the road ended. Tall waves of green grass swayed as we walked some fifty yards toward a ramshackle building. It looked fragile and dangerously close to collapse.

This property once belonged to a man named William Gatewood, and today it is recognized by the National Park Service as a site on the National Underground Railroad Network to Freedom. The Gatewood "plantation" is no picturesque antebellum homestead, hiding a history of slavery, but this spot was the scene of severe exploitation. Gatewood held several people in bondage before the Civil War, and one of them was Henry Bibb.

Henry Bibb (1815–54) entered the world as an enslaved person in Shelby County, Kentucky. By 1837 he was living on the Gatewood property and made his first escape in December of that year. After several subsequent attempts to flee and violent captures, Bibb finally secured his freedom. He arrived at Detroit in January of 1842 and sought an education, with the help of an abolitionist pastor.

Following his liberation Bibb began speaking out about slavery. During the spring of 1844 he lectured publicly for the first time in Adrian, Michigan.

Later he described this effort as "a narration of my own sufferings."[1] But Bibb was not content to tell a lurid tale. He wanted to interpret his experience, define its meaning, and fight the great wrongs done to him. Bibb moved to Canada in 1850 and founded an abolitionist newspaper.

The site of the William Gatewood plantation in Kentucky now hosts supervised digs in public archaeology. Guided by professionals from the Oldham County History Center, these excavations remove layers of earth and sift soil for clues to Bibb's story. The painstaking work at the Gatewood site has unearthed bits of pottery, nails, shards of glass, and other items from his life. Elizabeth and I were able to find a few small items during our brief visit there. For students of history, these digs peel back more than soil; time itself is stripped away.

Writing about the published memoirs left by Bibb and others, Toni Morrison once described her work as "a kind of literary archeology."[2] She explained, "On the basis of some information and a little bit of guess-work you journey to a site to see what remains were left behind and to reconstruct the world that these remains imply."[3] The written artifacts can even come alive through contemporary interpreters. Signs surface "so vividly and so compellingly that I acknowledge them as my route to a reconstruction of a world, to an exploration of an interior life that was not written and to the revelation of a kind of truth."[4] Literary archaeology does not create a world out of nothing, but it does listen for a world considered lost.

Fortunately, Henry Bibb wrote prodigiously in his later years. We may not know everything about his interior life, and we must guard against exaggerating our access to the workings of his mind. Yet Bibb's coming of age coincided with his speaking and writing. He wanted to tell us something. He wanted to be heard. It was no accident that Bibb's last major achievement came in the form of a newspaper named the *Voice of the Fugitive*. There was much to say, and he worked hard to say it.

Most of what we know about Bibb's early years was published in 1849 under the title *Narrative of the Life and Adventures of Henry Bibb*. The opening line reads, "I was born May 1815, of a slave mother, in Shelby County, Kentucky, and was claimed as the property of David White Esq."[5]

1. Bibb, *Narrative of the Life*, 178.
2. Morrison, "Site of Memory," 92.
3. Morrison, "Site of Memory," 92.
4. Morrison, "Site of Memory," 95.
5. Bibb, *Narrative of the Life*, 13.

However, Bibb did not restrict his memoir to the simple telling of biographical details. From the very first page he wove reflection regarding his experience through the narrative.

He noted that he was brought up in the counties of Shelby, Henry, Oldham, and Trimble, Kentucky, or rather *"flogged up"* in those places.[6] Expanding his reference, he observed, "For where I should have received moral, mental, and religious instruction, I received stripes without number, the object of which was to degrade and keep me in subordination."[7] He spent his entire life claiming and articulating a dignity that others attempted to deny him.

In 1833, at the age of eighteen, Bibb met a young woman named Malinda. The two were married, though without the legal protection enjoyed by other couples. Malinda was enslaved at the Gatewood plantation, and eventually Bibb joined her there. While working on the Gatewood estate, they welcomed a baby, Mary Frances. The three endured much abuse at Gatewood's place, and on December 25, 1837, Bibb left for Canada. When he reached Perrysburg, Ohio—near Toledo—he paused.[8]

Perrysburg was home to a settlement of African Americans, and Bibb spent the winter chopping wood. The next spring, with a little money saved, he resolved to return to Kentucky for his family. When he reached Cincinnati, Bibb took a steamboat toward the Gatewood plantation. He landed one evening about six miles from Bedford. Soon he surprised Malinda and made plans for her escape and the escape of Mary Frances. Mother and child were to meet him in Cincinnati later that week. Yet, while waiting, Bibb was betrayed and captured in Cincinnati. He was placed on a boat and anticipated a return to Gatewood's abuse. Instead, he was taken farther down river to Louisville. There his captors intended to sell him.[9]

In Louisville, Bibb managed to escape and scrambled back toward Bedford, some forty miles north and east. He met Malinda in the village, and she attempted to find a hiding place for him nearby. However, his escape had caused such an uproar in the area that he could not stay. His family was placed under increased surveillance, and so, with a heavy heart, Bibb said goodbye and journeyed toward Canada.[10]

6. Bibb, *Narrative of the Life*, 13 (emphasis original).
7. Bibb, *Narrative of the Life*, 13.
8. Bibb, *Narrative of the Life*, 33–56.
9. Bibb, *Narrative of the Life*, 57–71.
10. Bibb, *Narrative of the Life*, 72–80.

He met old friends in northern Ohio and waited several months, hoping that Malinda could make her escape and find him. She did not come. In July of 1839 he tried one more time to free his family. In secret Bibb arrived at the Gatewood estate and planned for the trip north. Again, he was captured.

A hostile mob discovered Bibb and surrounded a barn where he was hiding. The rabble bound his hands and robbed him of the few possessions he carried. Bibb later recalled, "In searching my pockets, they found my certificate from the Methodist E. Church, which had been given me by my classleader, testifying to my worthiness as a member of that church."[11] Worst of all, many in the mob were from the same church. In addition to taking his certificate, they stole fourteen dollars, a silver watch, a pocketknife, and a Bible. The rank hypocrisy and brutality of the assault spoke volumes. Bibb also noted that William Gatewood was a member of the same Methodist Episcopal Church to which he belonged.[12]

Bibb's spiritual commitment can be lost in the gripping twists and turns of his suffering and attempted escapes. Yet his unconquered faith is apparent throughout the narrative. As a young man Bibb met a poor white woman who offered to teach a Sabbath school for those in bondage. Books were secured, and the teaching commenced. Bibb wished to learn the Bible, but his nascent education was cut short when powerful people closed the school. Learning to read the Bible was considered an "incendiary" venture.[13]

The white establishment reserved for itself authority to interpret the Scriptures, and Bibb detested the self-serving arguments of proslavery apologists. The Bible was looted for passages that could be used to demand his subservience. He recalled the misapplication of Eph 6:5: "Servants be obedient to your masters." Bibb grieved the damage done by such manipulative handling of the Scriptures:

> This kind of preaching has driven thousands into infidelity. They view themselves as suffering unjustly under the lash, without friends, without protection of law or gospel, and the green eyed monster tyranny staring them in the face. They know that they are destined to die in that wretched condition, unless they are

11. Bibb, *Narrative of the Life*, 87.
12. Bibb, *Narrative of the Life*, 84–87.
13. Bibb, *Narrative of the Life*, 20.

delivered by the arm of Omnipotence. And they cannot believe or trust in such a religion, as above named.[14]

Given this disgusting system of injustice, it is amazing that Bibb or any other enslaved person would join a church.

Still, the same observations which condemned hypocritical professors of religion also referenced God's power to deliver. Bibb distinguished between those who posed as Christians and the authentic majesty of God. His refusal to consider God a domesticated tool of oppression remained with him throughout life.

Bibb's spiritual conviction was so strong that before marrying Malinda he talked with her about the importance of two matters: his faith and his desire to be free.[15] When preparing to leave slavery he "kneeled down before the Great I Am, and prayed for his aid and protection."[16] That Bibb found a home among Methodists probably reflects his limited choices in the region more than a doctrinal preference, but choice is a privilege seldom available to the oppressed. Bibb embraced his tradition and confronted its hypocrisy. In doing so, he lived a life more in keeping with the teachings of John Wesley than almost anyone else around him.

Following his capture by the mob near Bedford, Kentucky, Bibb was taken to Louisville and sold to a man named Madison Garrison (no relation to William Lloyd Garrison). Madison Garrison was a "soul driver" who traded in human beings the way others bought and sold produce or livestock.[17] During the fall of 1839, Bibb and his family were put on a boat and transported down the Ohio River, to the Mississippi, and farther south.

At Vicksburg, Mississippi, Bibb and many others were taken ashore. Garrison hoped to sell some of his captives. Bibb later recalled the degrading inspection he underwent to establish his market value. The invasive physical examination was disgusting. Yet he noted that the most rigorous scrutiny sought to determine intellectual skills. Those enslaved people who could read and write struck fear in oppressors. Bibb knew that his mind was both a gift from God and a delightfully dangerous possession.[18]

When the group arrived in New Orleans, Garrison hoped to sell Bibb and his family, but the purveyors of flesh would not purchase them.

14. Bibb, *Narrative of the Life*, 24.

15. Bibb, *Narrative of the Life*, 36.

16. Bibb, *Narrative of the Life*, 48.

17. Bibb, *Narrative of the Life*, 91.

18. Bibb, *Narrative of the Life*, 101–2.

Eventually they were sold to a cotton planter from Claiborne, Louisiana, by the name of Francis Whitfield. Bibb described Whitfield as someone who "looked like a saint" and yet acted "like the devil."[19] The terrible conditions, poor food, and physical abuse under Whitfield rivaled any Bibb experienced elsewhere. He and Malinda tried to escape with their daughter but were caught. A second child was born but died.

During this time Bibb labored in secret to learn to write. He found discarded scraps of paper and hid himself in the woods, perfecting his penmanship, but he struggled to understand what the letters meant. Only later would he master the whole art of writing, and, when he did, words poured out of his pen like an ever-flowing stream.[20]

Before long, Bibb was sold to a group of gamblers and separated from his family. They took him over the Red River, into Texas. Francis Whitfield was recognized as a deacon in the Baptist Church, and the gamblers who purchased Bibb were considered disreputable in the extreme. Yet Bibb remembered these shady characters for their relatively kind treatment of him. Again, professions of religious commitment meant little. How one acted toward others mattered.

Bibb even prevailed upon the gamblers to pass by Whitfield's plantation again. Perhaps they could purchase Malinda and Mary Frances. At least then the family would be together, but the contemptible old deacon refused. Bibb saw Malinda for the last time in December 1840.[21]

Finally, Bibb was sold to a man from the Cherokee nation, a person later described by Bibb as "reasonable" and "humane."[22] When this man died, Bibb made his move toward Canada. He traveled for days and took a horse to keep ahead of any potential pursuers. After arriving in Jefferson City, Missouri, he boarded a boat bound for St. Louis. At St. Louis he found passage on a boat headed to the Ohio River. From there Bibb worked his way back toward northwest Ohio. At long last, he arrived in Perrysburg, Ohio, in the fall of 1841. He continued on to Detroit (seventy miles farther north) during January of 1842.[23]

Detroit was a raucous outpost on the border with Canada. Echoes of French colonial presence, British occupation, and American expansion

19. Bibb, *Narrative of the Life*, 110.
20. Bibb, *Narrative of the Life*, 134–35.
21. Bibb, *Narrative of the Life*, 143–49.
22. Bibb, *Narrative of the Life*, 152.
23. Bibb, *Narrative of the Life*, 152–74.

pushed Native American communities deeper into the wilderness. Still, the collision of cultures, ethnicities, and religious identities offered cover for the escape of enslaved people across the river to freedom. In Detroit Bibb studied with a pastor named W. C. Monroe, but if this could be considered a formal education, it only lasted a few weeks. Almost all of Bibb's later prowess as a speaker and writer was self-developed.[24]

The rugged perseverance that brought Bibb to Detroit did not come easily. Every part of society told him that he did not belong, that he was marginally human. However, Bibb reminded the readers of his autobiography that public opinion and human law were always against him. No matter. He knew that he was created for dignity. This truth arose from his very nature, and he borrowed language from the Declaration of Independence to explain it. Such freedom was revealed to him by "the inevitable laws of nature's God."[25]

Bibb acknowledged that he was, like all people, susceptible to misfortune, but he could not accept those restrictions which denied him the right to defend "life, liberty, and happiness."[26] He embraced the founding principles of America's revolution, but he railed against the inconsistent practice of those principles. Just as he called out people who professed a Christian commitment while failing to live its teachings, he named America's hypocrisy.

Abusive civil codes, statutes, and legislation might try to keep Bibb from his destiny, but they were judged by the authority of God. He may not have expressed this reasoning with the same meticulous detail wielded by Luther Lee and others. But his struggle bore a living testimony to the supremacy of the divine law.

A Narration of My Own Sufferings

Bibb's arrival in Detroit coincided with wider developments among the American abolitionist movement. During the early 1830s antislavery forces realized the need for a nationwide organization to provide coordinated advocacy. The American Anti-Slavery Society was formed in 1833 and brought a diverse cast of actors together. Many of the participants were evangelical church folk, revivalist Christians who united a

24. Bibb, *Narrative of the Life*, 174.
25. Bibb, *Narrative of the Life*, 17.
26. Bibb, *Narrative of the Life*, 18.

conversion-oriented faith and the demands of social justice. Others were less committed to traditional theological beliefs and criticized organized religion for its complicity with slavery.

These two constituencies tended to radiate from different regions of the country. The more evangelical believers were strong in New York State and the Old Northwest; those with unconventional theologies often lived in New England. By 1840 the American Anti-Slavery Society split. Established church folk left and founded the American and Foreign Anti-Slavery Society. The original group was then dominated by members from New England.

Over the years historians have often described those with traditional theological convictions as "moderates" in the cause against slavery. Those who worked outside religious organizations are typically described as "radicals." This framework has led to the assumption that a faith commitment tempered concern for justice and that those who thumbed their noses at Christian doctrine were automatically more inclusive and affirming. The presumption, however, says more about later interpretive views than it does about the antislavery movement.[27]

Traditional believers did defend organized religion, and some also failed to support women's leadership in the abolitionist movement. Yet others were heartfelt exponents of the gospel and advocates for absolute equality—regarding both race and gender. Luther Lee was one such evangelical abolitionist. Moreover, New Englanders lauded as unqualified prophets for justice were not always consistent witnesses. This was especially the case when eastern abolitionists expressed a suffocating paternalism toward formerly enslaved people.

The experience of Frederick Douglass (1818–95) is revealing. When Douglass first freed himself from slavery, he found a home among New England abolitionists. In 1841 he joined William Lloyd Garrison's Massachusetts Anti-Slavery Society. Douglass brought credibility to the movement as someone who endured the horrors of slavery. He soon joined the speaking circuit and told his story to countless people. The predominantly white audiences were hungry for his accounts of suffering and cruelty in the South.[28]

Garrison and others were captivated by Douglass, but they only wanted to hear a tale of woe. They did not want to hear Douglass reflect upon his

27. One version of this interpretive framework can be seen in Emerson and Smith, *Divided by Faith.*

28. Douglass, *My Bondage*, 366.

experience or chart a course in the fight against slavery. He was to be an exhibit, a piece of evidence for the prosecution, against bondage. Douglass recalled, "I was generally introduced as a 'chattel'—a 'thing'—a piece of southern 'property'—the chairman assuring the audience that it could speak."[29] Yet the speaking featured was strictly controlled by white handlers.

Douglass knew himself to be the intellectual equal of any person. He desired to elaborate upon his experience, and he began analyzing and denouncing slavery. At this his Garrisonian "friends" took him aside and corrected him. He was to refrain from argument. They would make the case against slavery. Douglass was there to narrate a story of victimization. John A. Collins of the Massachusetts Anti-Slavery Society often introduced the speakers at events. Douglass later recalled the instructions he received from Collins: "'Give us the facts,' said Collins, 'we will take care of the philosophy.'"[30] The irony of such degrading treatment escaped the awareness of most self-congratulatory "radicals."

Not long after Frederick Douglass entered the strange world of anti-slavery oratory, Henry Bibb found himself in similar circumstances. Since early 1842 Bibb had made Detroit his home. He even received correspondence there from William Gatewood and in the spring of 1844 responded through a strong letter, articulating his dignity and self-determination: "I thank God that I am not property now, but am regarded as a man like yourself, and although I live far north, I am enjoying a comfortable living by my own industry. If you should ever chance to be traveling this way, and will call on me, I will use you better than you did me while you held me as a slave."[31] Bibb was willing to interact with Gatewood but only under conditions of absolute equality.

In May of 1844 Bibb arrived at a critical moment. He was asked to speak about his experiences in slavery. The address was given in Adrian, Michigan—one year before Laura Haviland and her family went through their crucible of epidemic and death there. Bibb wrote, "The first time that I ever spoke before a public audience, was to give a narration of my own sufferings and adventures, connected with slavery. I commenced in the village of Adrian, State of Michigan, May, 1844."[32] Soon he became a regular lecturer for the Michigan State Anti-Slavery Society.

29. Douglass, *My Bondage*, 366.
30. Douglass, *My Bondage*, 367.
31. Bibb, *Narrative of the Life*, 176.
32. Bibb, *Narrative of the Life*, 178.

We do not know if Bibb experienced the same kind of paternalism while lecturing that Frederick Douglass endured. Yet Bibb did describe his task as offering a "narration of my own sufferings."[33] He certainly inherited the same burden as Douglass—that of telling his story to predominantly white audiences. One thing is clear: When Bibb entered the arena of antislavery speakers, he took a giant step forward in finding and sharing his voice.

All of this happened when a new abolitionist political party was growing throughout parts of the North and especially in Michigan. As a response to William Lloyd Garrison's avoidance of political involvement and legislative advocacy, some formed the Liberty Party. Like the regional loyalties of the Foreign and American Anti-Slavery Society, the Liberty Party was especially strong in New York State and the Old Northwest.

This political action wing of the abolitionist movement began in 1840. Many trace its origin to a meeting in Peterboro, New York, between Gerrit Smith (1797–1874), William Goodell (1792–1878), and James G. Birney (1792–1857) during February of that year.[34] The first Liberty Party convention met in Albany, New York, on April 1, 1840. Throughout much of the 1840s Henry Bibb served as a speaker on behalf of Liberty Party candidates for office.

In the fall of 1844, Bibb and a colleague spent more than two months lecturing throughout Michigan. He remembered, "Our meetings were generally appointed in small log cabins, school houses, among the farmers, which were some times crowded full; and where they had no horse teams, it was often the case that there would be four or five ox teams come, loaded down with men, women and children, to attend our meetings."[35] His audiences included both committed abolitionists and those drawn by simple curiosity.

During October of 1844 Bibb's name appeared within the *Signal of Liberty*, published in Ann Arbor, Michigan. He had recently spoken in a nearby town, and one witness filed a report: "When it is considered that he has been regarded as a mere chattel or thing, and writhed under the lash of inhuman taskmasters, nearly all his life, entirely deprived of the advantages of an education, the case [sic] and fluency with which he speaks,

---

33. Bibb, *Narrative of the Life*, 178.
34. Dann, *Practical Dreamer*, 320.
35. Bibb, *Narrative of the Life*, 180–81.

and the intelligence which he exhibits, are truly astonishing."[36] The writer concluded by predicting that many voters attached to the reigning political powers would shift their allegiance to the Liberty Party.

Bibb's gripping story led to rising stature in Michigan antislavery circles. Most were transfixed by his account, but some doubted its truthfulness. James G. Birney, the Liberty Party's presidential candidate for 1840 and 1844, heard Bibb speak in February of 1845 and questioned his authenticity.[37] This put Bibb in an understandably awkward position. Not only did he have to defend himself against proslavery ideologues, he also had to acquit himself among those who claimed to be advocates for justice.

Birney was born in Danville, Kentucky, and later moved to Alabama. He became a noted planter and politician. At one point he owned several enslaved people. During the 1830s Birney underwent a crisis of conscience and a change of conviction. He then devoted himself to immediate abolition. By the 1840s he lived in Bay City, Michigan, and was regarded as one of the nation's leading political abolitionists.

The proximity of Birney to Henry Bibb might have led to a dynamic partnership, but that did not happen. Instead, Bibb was pressured to substantiate his story. He confronted Birney in a letter and wrote, "I am now trying to collect some facts to prove the reality of my Narrative."[38] Bibb also submitted to an examination and interrogation by the Detroit Liberty Association. This organization created a formal committee of investigation to authenticate or deny Bibb's claims. Even letters from Southern plantation owners were taken as valid testimony. Later that spring Bibb was exonerated of all suspicion, and statements of endorsement were issued. Many such declarations were published in the opening pages of Bibb's *Narrative* when it was released in 1849.

Those calling themselves Bibb's friends missed the hypocrisy of presuming veracity from white witnesses, even those who profited from slavery, while doubting his word. Glowing vindications were certainly well-intended, but why did he bear such an unreasonable burden of proof in the first place? Few white abolitionists were scrutinized with such rigor. There was a disgusting double standard evident in the whole painful experience. Those with established power anointed themselves gatekeepers for the movement.

36. "Mr. Bibb's Lectures," 100.
37. Cooper, "'Doing Battle in Freedom's Cause,'" 62.
38. Dumond, *Letters of James Gillespie Birney*, 2:928.

Bibb continued lecturing, and some committed to support him through a unique form of compensation. In return for his labors, friends would pledge to find and restore to him his wife and child.[39] However, the family reunion never happened, even though Bibb attempted to find Malinda and Mary Frances one more time.[40]

Henry Bibb was a persistent warrior in the cause of freedom, and he did not let mistreatment by friends or by enemies keep him from articulating a conscientious vision. In October of 1846 he published an opinion piece in the *Signal of Liberty*. This carefully structured essay bore the intriguing title: "Consistency Is a Gem." Not content to narrate his personal story alone, Bibb developed an argument for abolitionist action. The idea of consistency was central to any successful campaign. Those working for change should keep focused and not turn aside from the main task: "Friends of *Liberty*, be true to what you profess—meet often together and discuss your principles."[41] Yet discussion was only the beginning.

Consistent action was required, too. Bibb indicted the followers of William Lloyd Garrison, and despite his unfair experience with some Liberty Party leaders, he agreed that political action was crucial. Garrisonians folded up their arms and foolishly refused to vote against slavery. Liberty Party activists went to the ballot box and deposited votes for freedom. Bibb concluded by charging his readers, "Consistent action is the key to emancipation."[42] This statement was no cliché.

By addressing both principle and action, Bibb integrated two things that were rarely mentioned in simple narratives of abuse. He wrote not only about his experience but about the meaning of his experience and what that experience could offer. He wrote about ideas and their motivating power, and then he urged action in conformity with those ideas. Bibb's writing was advancing beyond the basic appeal of story to analysis of that story and a determination to make a difference. He certainly possessed a voice now, but he also supercharged that voice by using it to express life-giving principles and by imploring concrete steps toward justice.

39. Bibb, *Narrative of the Life*, 185.
40. Bibb, *Narrative of the Life*, 188–89.
41. Bibb, "Consistency Is a Gem," 93.
42. Bibb, "Consistency Is a Gem," 93.

Henry Bibb (1815–1854), shown here in 1847, indicted
his fellow Methodists for tolerating slavery.

Image Courtesy of the National Portrait Gallery,
Smithsonian Institution

Soon Bibb embarked on a new project. The "Bibles for Slaves" campaign
was launched to provide Scriptures for enslaved people and formerly enslaved
people. His robust support of the venture first appeared in a report published
on June 2, 1847, in *The Emancipator*, a prominent abolitionist newspaper af-
filiated with the Liberty Party. Joshua Leavitt (1794–1873), the paper's editor,
partnered with Bibb to raise funds for purchase of the Bibles.

That Bibb would publish his appeal in *The Emancipator* made perfect
sense, but three weeks later his letter was circulated in *The Liberator*, William Lloyd Garrison's paper. The appearance of Bibb's plea in *The Liberator*

was not an endorsement of the campaign. Garrison shared the letter and then ridiculed the project. Bibb's communication reported on the annual meeting of the American Anti-Slavery Society. During this gathering Garrison and Frederick Douglass sponsored a formal statement opposing the "Bibles for Slaves" campaign. It read, in part, "We regard the project of giving the Bible to the slaves, which has been started in Massachusetts by those who claim to be Abolitionists, as delusive, and calculated to retard the Anti-Slavery cause."[43] Among the American Anti-Slavery Society, there were very few defenders of the campaign.

The Garrisonians attacked the venture as a weak initiative that played into the hands of oppressors. Bibb begged to differ and argued that if enslaved people were able to read the Bible, "there would not be power enough in all the South to hold them in bondage."[44] The conflict over this specific project reflected the broader divide between Garrisonians and the Liberty Party. The unorthodox religious views of Garrison and his followers diluted their interest in the Bible. The more traditional theological convictions of political abolitionists fit nicely with the campaign.

For Bibb, the debate highlighted several defining characteristics of his antislavery philosophy. First, he denied that the Scriptures, when genuinely interpreted, supported any form of injustice. He expressed absolute disdain for Southern ideologues who tried to use the Bible to justify slavery. Second, Bibb's own liberation was grounded in learning to read the Bible. The sheer power of literacy remained a core tenet of his work. Finally, he was his own person. Just as he would not let proslavery manipulators get away with hijacking the Bible, he did not feel obligated to concede his principles when pressured by Northern skeptics. Henry Bibb was never in anyone's pocket.

Our Warfare Lies in the Field of Thought

In 2019 historian Amy Lewis published an essay bearing the title "Who'll Speak for Malinda? Alternate Narratives of Freedom in *The Life and Adventures of Henry Bibb*."[45] Lewis probed what it means for readers of Bibb's *Narrative* to consider the experience of his wife, Malinda. She remained in slavery following Bibb's emancipation, and we have no direct testimony

43. Bibb, Letter to the Editor, 107.
44. Bibb, Letter to the Editor, 107.
45. Lewis, "Who'll Speak for Malinda?," 255–76.

from her that would indicate how she processed the crushing injustices of her life. Who speaks for Malinda? How is she to be respected in the hearing of Bibb's story?

The question takes on additional gravity when we consider that Bibb eventually considered his marriage with Malinda to be broken and at an end. How did events unfold? How did Bibb represent himself through these changes? How might Malinda have described the story?

There are more questions than answers here. Behind all the brokenness is the limited agency or choice available to enslaved people. Bibb's marriage to Malinda was perpetually under threat by the arbitrary abuses of slavery. A covenant unrecognized by civil law required almost superhuman persistence. When abolitionists promised to help Bibb retrieve his family, there appeared to be hope for reunion. He traveled to Madison, Indiana—ten miles from the Gatewood property—and heard disappointing news. He wrote, "No sooner had I landed in Madison, than I learned, on inquiry, and from good authority, that my wife was living in a state of adultery with her master, and had been for the last three years."[46] This description implies that Malinda entered into a long-standing, consensual relationship with someone else, while still married to Bibb. The truth is more complicated.

As an enslaved person, Malinda would not have enjoyed the typical forms of prerogative suggested by the term "adultery." She possessed little if any power in a relationship with someone claiming to own her. For Bibb to describe Malinda as living in adultery might excuse him from obligation to her, but it was certainly not the whole truth. Nor was it fair.

The sticky and poignant end to Bibb's marriage highlights another contemptible dynamic of slavery: the ongoing inequality between those who do and those who do not attain freedom. Bibb wrote his own life after slavery. He was able to read, write, and define himself. Yet Malinda did not have the same autonomy at her disposal. Almost everything we know about her is derived from Bibb. It is not exactly the case that Bibb developed his voice at the expense of Malinda, but the literacy that accompanied his growth shaped the narrative around his marriage. We only know his side of the story.

In May of 1847 Bibb attended an antislavery gathering in New York City where he met Mary E. Miles. The two formed a bond and became engaged. They waited a year and were married in June of 1848. Miles (1820–77) was a free person of color from Rhode Island. Between 1842 to 1844 she attended the Lexington Normal School in Massachusetts and aspired to be

46. Bibb, *Narrative of the Life*, 188.

a teacher. During November of 1845 she moved to Albany, New York, and pursued her vocation. Miles then taught school in Cincinnati.[47]

Mary Miles Bibb was her own person. She had crafted a unique identity before meeting Henry and was admired by many. She was disciplined, educated, and possessed a burning sense of mission. The two lived rather separate lives from 1848 to 1850. During this time Henry Bibb made quite a tour of the New England lecture circuit.

In 1849 the *Narrative of the Life and Adventures of Henry Bibb* was published. Lucius C. Matlack (1816–83) wrote a glowing introduction. Matlack was a founder of the Wesleyan Methodist Connection and a close friend of Luther Lee. He had released *The History of American Slavery and Methodism, from 1780–1849* that same year.

However, Bibb's association with Methodism was not limited to its abolitionist leaders. The last few paragraphs of the *Narrative* confronted those who betrayed John Wesley's legacy. Bibb reminded readers that many of his abusers had been Methodists: "A. Sibley was a Methodist exhorter of the M. E. Church in good standing. J. Sibley was a class-leader in the same church; and Wm. Gatewood was also an acceptable member of the same church. Is this Christianity? Is it honest or right?"[48] Bibb would not let his church off the hook.

Between 1849 and 1850 Bibb wrote four books: his autobiography, two historical studies, and a song book. Then the so-called Compromise of 1850 came as an intolerable jolt. Bibb and many others prepared to leave for Canada. Bibb had freed himself from slavery without legal redemption or release. But his emigration was not an escape, and contrary to assumptions by later interpreters, he was not particularly afraid of capture. He was done with American hypocrisy.

The Fugitive Slave legislation became law in September 1850. By November people of color gathered in Sandwich, Canada West (now Windsor, Ontario) to form a society that would welcome and support expatriates from the United States. Bibb was a key figure in this movement.

He participated in conventions dedicated to the cause of freedom and supported a formal resolution that invoked the Declaration of Independence's second paragraph: "We hold these truths to be self eviden [*sic*], that all men are created equal, and that they are endowed by their Creator with certain inalienable rights, and that among these are, Life, Liberty,

47. Cooper, "'Doing Battle in Freedom's Cause,'" 448–51.

48. Bibb, *Narrative of the Life*, 203.

and the pursuit of Happiness."[49] This same resolution declared that "the last Session of the Congress of the United States of America repudiated this principle, by the passing of what is called the fugitive slave law, and thereby proved themselves to be hypocrits [*sic*] and infidels to their own doctrine."[50] As Bibb and others saw things, they had not left their country behind so much as their country had lost itself.

While perhaps not said in so many words, Bibb understood America to be an idea and not simply a location on the map. If America would not be true to itself on one side of the Detroit River, he would nurture its flame on the other.

This he set about doing and along with others established a settlement where people desiring freedom could purchase land, build homes, and learn to read and write. A resolution called for the creation of a printing press and for a publication that would promote the settlement. The language was stirring: "As we struggle against opinions, our warfare lies in the field of thought."[51] Again, ideas mattered, and a medium for the exchange of ideas and the advancement of them was necessary.

This determination to publish a newspaper bore fruit on January 1, 1851, when the *Voice of the Fugitive* appeared. Bibb edited the paper until less than a year before his death in 1854, and there is evidence that Mary Bibb contributed generously to the project. She undoubtedly served as an editor for major periods of the venture.[52]

The first issue articulated the publication's aims: "We expect, by the aid of a good Providence, to advocate the cause of human liberty in the true meaning of that term. We shall advocate the immediate and unconditional abolition of chattel slavery every where, but especially on the American soil."[53] Bibb had not forsaken his native land. On the contrary, he hoped to save it.

Soon advocates from diverse backgrounds rallied to the settlement. This was the period when Laura Haviland joined the Bibbs for a stint of school teaching. The *Voice of the Fugitive* has been called Henry Bibb's "crowning achievement," and this is certainly true.[54] For someone who

49. "Fugitive Slaves in Canada West," 2.
50. "Fugitive Slaves in Canada West," 2.
51. "Fugitive Slaves in Canada West," 2.
52. Cooper, "'Doing Battle in Freedom's Cause,'" 452.
53. "Fugitive Slaves in Canada West," 2.
54. Cooper, "'Doing Battle in Freedom's Cause,'" 299.

dug himself out of slavery and then developed the ability to read and write, the paper represented a stunning accomplishment. Bibb was not only eloquent in word and pen, he also commanded respect as an editor of expression offered by others. He became a shaper, a midwife really, of talent drawn to the cause.

However, the *Voice of the Fugitive* was more than an intellectual victory. It was a vehicle for supporting the day-to-day welfare of people leaving slavery. Plans were made, funds were raised, and tasks were assigned among the mission of finding homes and promoting literacy. Even though Bibb's personal voice was given concrete form in the published *Voice*, he knew that authentic speaking is not satisfied with simply making noise. True speech has a purpose.

During more recent times historians of slavery have shifted away from the term "fugitive." The word suggests criminality.[55] Those seeking freedom may have been in violation of distorted human laws, but they were certainly not in violation of the divine law. Bibb understood this more than anyone around him, and still he was not bothered by renegade language if it could be deployed to affirm human dignity. This he did in the *Voice of the Fugitive*.

One subject addressed in Bibb's paper was the residual tolerance of slavery among northern Methodism. Even today many presume that following the split of mainline Methodism in 1844, northern expressions of the movement were clear from bondage. This is not quite so. Bibb let it be known that the Methodist Episcopal Church (North) remained complicit in slavery.

The June 18, 1851, issue of the *Voice* carried a lengthy article with the provocative title "Is the M. E. Church of the North Pro-Slavery?" Bibb cited the American and Foreign Anti-Slavery Society Report for May 1851.

That document included a damning note: "Of the 219,563 slaves owned in the Methodist Church, the greater portion by far are owned in the Church South. The Church North, however, is by no means guiltless of the blood of the innocent. She has her churches in the South in which slaves are held, and the owners are in good standing."[56] This same report observed, "Much remains to be done in the M. E. Church North even, before it comes up to the standard of its illustrious founder, whose most matured sentiment, fearlessly announced, was, 'Slavery is the sum of all villainies.'"[57] Bibb's June 18

---

55. Washington, *Sojourner Truth's America*, ix.

56. "Annual Report of the American and Foreign Anti-Slavery Society," 56.

57. "Annual Report of the American and Foreign Anti-Slavery Society," 41.

column reminded readers that "we speak from experience upon the subject for we have been bought and sold by the M. E. Church while a member of that body."[58] Throughout his writing Bibb underscored the way honesty was a necessary component of social justice.

The newspaper business before the American Civil War was a precarious game. Publications often lasted less than a year. There was machinery to buy and maintain, staff to pay, and families to provide for. There was the grinding task of cultivating good writing by contributors and the ever-present need for funding. Subscriptions could underwrite much, but other sources of income were coveted as well. These obstacles were even more daunting for communities of color.

After almost a year of publication, Bibb looked back to the crisis of 1850: "Hundreds of our brethren were flying daily to Canada to escape the claws of the American Eagle, which wages incessant warfare against the law of God and the happiness of our people."[59] The law of God remained the ultimate standard, and Bibb certainly expressed sadness over the betrayal of American ideals. But he also celebrated efforts to keep that dream alive.

In our day, so many equate criticism of America's behavior with an attack on its foundations. If one wants America to be better, to be more just, that is often mischaracterized as a lack of patriotism. If one holds out a mirror to the church and names inconsistencies or sin, that person is often labeled a malcontent. Yet smear tactics and victim-blaming are tools of those who refuse to admit that their power has corrupted them. Henry Bibb did not hate America when he left for Canada. He grieved for America. He did not take delight in confronting Methodism. He wanted his movement to live up to its founding vision. We have much to learn from him and his ability to experience brutalizing marginalization while also encouraging the better angels of his world.

The *Voice of the Fugitive* soldiered on until October of 1853, when a fire of suspicious origin burned the operation to the ground.[60] The tragedy devastated Bibb, and we will never know whether he might have regained his literary poise over the long haul. Before too many months passed, he was ill. During July of 1854 friends expressed concern for Bibb's health and visited him. He died after a "fever" in the early hours of Tuesday, August 1.

58. "Is the M. E. Church," 2.

59. "To Our Readers," 2.

60. "The Fugitive Burned," 171.

Over the years the first of August has been honored as "Emancipation Day" in many parts of the globe. The act to abolish slavery throughout the British Empire was enacted in 1833, and August 1, 1834, became the day this policy was implemented. Celebrations marking the anniversary along the Detroit River were underway in 1854 when Bibb's longtime friend, George de Baptiste (1815–75), broke the sad news to others.[61] Many of the ceremonies paused to eulogize Bibb. August 1 would take on added meaning going forward.

Remains of the William Gatewood plantation near Bedford, Kentucky yield clues to the early life of Henry Bibb.

Photo by Christopher P. Momany

61. Cooper, "'Doing Battle in Freedom's Cause,'" 477.

For all his dogged efforts to express himself, hints of inaccessibility still surround the life of Bibb. Those of us who scratch in the dirt on a crude Kentucky plantation might come up with fragments of evidence, but we know that much remains out of reach. The call from that beyond is strong and tempts us to construct missing parts, but the call also warns us that the story we desire is not ours. The story belongs, exclusively, to Henry Bibb. It is, after all, *his* voice.

Chapter VI

GILBERT HAVEN

The Higher Law

My Mother and My Bible Made Me an Abolitionist

IN 2011, THE GENERAL Commission on Archives and History of the United Methodist Church, located in Madison, New Jersey, received over one thousand documents from descendants of Bishop Gilbert Haven. Most striking is a letter written by Haven to abolitionist John Brown, dated November 18, 1859. This was roughly one month after the uprising in Harpers Ferry, Virginia. On November 2 Brown had been sentenced to die, and within weeks he was executed. Haven's letter was written while Brown awaited his fate.[1]

The letter may be a draft of one sent to Brown, or it may be the intended document that was never sent. Its contents reveal Haven's glowing support for Brown and his cause. The opening sentence reads, "I take the liberty to send you a copy of a discourse I preached on Sabbath Evening Nov. 6th."[2] That discourse was undoubtedly a sermon later published in several venues. Haven delivered the address as an exoneration of Brown and as an encouragement while he steeled himself for martyrdom.

The sermon was given at the Harvard Street Methodist Episcopal Church, Cambridge, Massachusetts, and first published in Boston's *Daily Evening Traveller*, November 15, 1859.[3] The next year it was one of several

---

1. Patterson, "Discovery," 233–36.
2. Letter from Gilbert Haven to John Brown, November 18, 1859, in Haven, Papers.
3. Gravely, *Gilbert Haven Methodist Abolitionist*, 65.

addresses and essays published in a volume by James Redpath: *Echoes of Harper's Ferry*.

The crescendo of Haven's sermon confronted ways civil law marginalized African Americans. He listed shameful violations of human rights and pointed to the Supreme Court's Dred Scott decision of 1857. Haven thundered, "My God, what a decree! Let us obey God rather than man."[4] Surely divine justice carried more authority than the twisted edicts of human law, even those delivered by the United States Supreme Court. By 1859, the invocation of a duty to "obey God rather than man" was standard in abolitionist circles.

This language came from Acts 5:29. Scripture records how religious authorities forbade Peter and company from proclaiming Jesus, to which they responded, "We ought to obey God rather than men" (KJV). Proslavery apologists often quoted Rom 13 and its requirement that Christians honor civil authority, but abolitionists expressed a rejoinder in the form of Acts 5:29. Human laws may attempt to excuse slavery, but God's authority demanded freedom and dignity.

The employment of Acts 5:29 to condemn bondage had featured prominently in an 1842 sermon preached by Elijah Lovejoy's brother Owen. Owen Lovejoy was a Congregational pastor serving in Princeton, Illinois, when he delivered his legendary address on "The Supremacy of the Divine Law."[5] This sermon foreshadowed Luther Lee's 1846 effort by the same title. Lee grounded his argument in Acts 23:29, but Lovejoy's discourse was straight out of Acts 5:29. In November of 1859 Gilbert Haven offered a tribute to John Brown, rooted in Acts 5:29, that would have made Lovejoy and Lee proud.

Haven was the oldest son and fifth child of Gilbert and Hannah (Burrill) Haven, born on September 19, 1821, in Malden, Massachusetts. This was the very cradle of the American Revolution—north of Boston and but five miles from Bunker Hill. Throughout his sermons and essays Haven would reference the Battle of Bunker Hill as a lodestar for liberty-loving people. The countryside surrounding Malden was featured in Longfellow's 1861 poem, "Paul Revere's Ride." This embellished ballad not only celebrated revolutionary courage, it also connected the ideas of 1775 with the antislavery cause as America stumbled toward civil war. Haven understood

4. Redpath, *Echoes of Harper's Ferry*, 139.

5. Moore and Moore, *His Brother's Blood*, 19–24.

the relevance of his regional history and mined it for wisdom when he grew into an unyielding abolitionist.

Haven's parents were established Congregationalists, but by 1823, they had both joined the Methodist Episcopal Church.[6] The combination of Puritan and Methodist principles grounded the entire family and its values. A commitment to integrity, devotion to God, and public service formed an unwritten curriculum in the Haven household. Young Gilbert drank from this well throughout his religious upbringing and during his schooling.[7]

Once, at the local grammar school, a teacher lashed out at the lone African American student, a girl, striking her for some insignificant infraction. Haven confronted the teacher. When he returned home his mother insisted that the girl was just as good as him. He had done the right thing. Later in life he claimed that his mother and the Bible made him an abolitionist.[8]

This did not mean that young Haven was without fault or innately beyond the racism of his time. On one occasion he made a demeaning comment to an African American woman, and she took him to task. Calling his name, she expressed shock at receiving such disrespectful speech from him.[9] In his shame and remorse he promised that he would never act that way again, and as far as we know, he kept his word. Gilbert Haven came from good people and demonstrated much potential, but, even at that, it took a village to shape his character.

When Haven was fourteen, he worked in one of Malden's dry goods stores. He liked books and made time to read them. His sister, Bethiah, was known for her intellectual gifts, and she tutored Gilbert in Latin and French. He chafed under the limited opportunities in Malden and sought a more formal education. During the spring of 1839, he entered the Wesleyan Academy in Wilbraham, Massachusetts, almost ninety miles west of his home.

The Wesleyan Academy was founded in 1818 in New Market, New Hampshire, and was relocated to Massachusetts during 1825. The school thrived under sponsorship from the Methodist Episcopal Church and distinguished itself as an environment devoted to deep piety. One might think that Haven's religious background and hunger for learning would bloom

6. Gravely, *Gilbert Haven Methodist Abolitionist*, 15.

7. Gravely, *Gilbert Haven Methodist Abolitionist*, 15–17.

8. Prentice, *Life of Gilbert Haven*, 21–22.

9. Prentice, *Life of Gilbert Haven*, 24.

in such a place, but his early pursuits in Wilbraham were neither spiritual nor scholastic. He made a name for himself as one of the least disciplined students and excelled at the diversions of social life.[10]

When a revival broke out in Wilbraham, Haven demonstrated little interest. His attitude was later described as "partly one of dislike but mainly of indifference."[11] He did possess a flair for argument and appreciated good public speaking, so he attended some of the services. Haven was more curious than committed, but in listening, he was convicted and converted. He met Jesus in a most profound manner, and it changed his life.

Haven wrote a letter to his parents, expressing excitement for his new beginning and regret for past frivolity: "I cannot describe my feelings; they were a mixture of joy and sorrow, of gladness and mourning."[12] This took place in October 1839, and his sister, Bethiah, was languishing from poor health. He returned home in November, and his spiritual awakening inspired a renewal of family relationships. About a month later, Bethiah passed into God's kingdom.

During March of 1840, Haven became a clerk in the store owned by L. W. and C. H. Nichols of Boston. The business was tedious, and his employers were difficult. A year later he left to work in a carpet store. This new situation suited Haven, and he became an admired salesperson. The long hours threatened to distract him from proper spiritual pursuits, but Haven managed to worship regularly and attend prayer meetings. And he read. He read *The Life of Mrs. Mary Fletcher* (an early Methodist saint) and Thomas à Kempis (*The Imitation of Christ*) and Asa Mahan's *Scripture Doctrine of Christian Perfection*.[13] Mahan's treatise on sanctification, published in Boston in 1839, had a profound effect on the entire Methodist movement. Haven's reading broadened and deepened his interior life, but it also addressed a burning question: How was he to find his vocation, his very purpose?

Haven was never fully satisfied with his employment, and his intellectual curiosity would not let him rest. He returned to the Wesleyan Academy in March of 1842 and prepared in earnest for college. His habits were different than those adopted when he first lived in Wilbraham. Now he rose at 5:00 a.m. for exercise and then engaged in prayer at 6:00. He read Cicero with a diligence that would exhaust most people and translated Virgil. He

10. Prentice, *Life of Gilbert Haven*, 29–31.

11. Prentice, *Life of Gilbert Haven*, 32.

12. Quoted in Prentice, *Life of Gilbert Haven*, 33.

13. Prentice, *Life of Gilbert Haven*, 43.

studied Greek and rarely wasted time that could be spent on improvement.[14] Haven had always been a dynamo, and now he applied that energy to mental activity. Scholarship was not leisure. It was meaningful work.

Haven entered the first-year class at Wesleyan University in Middle-town, Connecticut, during the fall of 1842. The university had been founded in 1831 and was a fine academic institution. It was, however, not a place devoted to the antislavery cause. In fact, early leadership of the school took a decidedly dim view of abolitionists. Stephen Olin (1797–1851) served as president of Wesleyan during Haven's years on campus. The president was a preacher par excellence, but he had dubious ties to slavery. Born in Vermont, Olin spent several years in South Carolina and Georgia before leading Randolph-Macon College in Ashland, Virginia, during the 1830s. While living in the South, he claimed ownership of enslaved people.[15] Olin's compromising attitude toward slavery remained with him when he returned to New England and took up duties at Wesleyan. Haven's budding human rights awareness was not nurtured by college officials.

No matter. Haven learned to thrive despite the environment around him. This was the same autumn when Luther Lee accepted a preaching assignment in Andover, Massachusetts, and Orange Scott led a meeting with colleagues who were contemplating secession from the Methodist Episcopal Church. The centers of power in the academy and the church might have been arrayed against antislavery sentiment, but there were pockets of resistance growing, especially in New England, New York State, and Michigan.

Haven was a younger colleague of these experienced Wesleyan abolitionists. Yet what he lacked in years was overcome by zeal and blazing intellect, and he never considered his studies a diversion from larger moral commitments. He plunged into further reading of Virgil, devoured Ovid, and worked his way through the Greek New Testament. He also appreciated the natural beauty of his surroundings and mentioned it in letters to friends and family.[16]

There was always a self-directed quality to Haven's education. He read far and wide, beyond the curriculum of Wesleyan University. His journal notes that he read Ralph Waldo Emerson's *Essays*, Thomas Carlyle's *The French Revolution*, and Samuel Taylor Coleridge's *Works*. He enjoyed a host

14. Prentice, *Life of Gilbert Haven*, 48–49.

15. Gravely, *Gilbert Haven Methodist Abolitionist*, 21–23.

16. Prentice, *Life of Gilbert Haven*, 51–53.

of devotional classics, too.[17] Emerson traveled to Middletown during commencement week of 1845 and delivered a lecture on the "Function of the Scholar." The next winter, when Haven was teaching at Chelsea Point, Massachusetts, he attended talks given by the sage of Concord in Boston.[18]

While a student at Wesleyan University, Haven asked his family to send him abolitionist literature. He placed these materials in the campus reading room and worked at bringing fellow students to the antislavery struggle, with limited success. He was not confused about his loyalties and began to teach in a Sabbath school among Middletown's African American community.[19]

During February of 1846, Haven joined several clergy leaders in organizing a "Religious Anti-Slavery Convention," held at the Marlboro' Chapel in Boston. This church building, on Washington Street, became celebrated for hosting a series of landmark events in the abolitionist movement. Some years earlier Asa Mahan delivered his iconic lectures on sanctification at Marlboro' Chapel, and these very talks were subsequently published as the *Scripture Doctrine of Christian Perfection.*

Haven and his colleagues issued a call for the convention based on their conviction "that the Gospel properly administered is the great charter of human freedom and equal rights."[20] Most sponsors of the event and crafters of its statement were established clergy, from a wide variety of backgrounds. Haven had yet to graduate from college, but that milestone was soon within reach.

Commencement at Wesleyan University arrived on August 5, 1846, and the day's program featured a slate of assigned speeches by the graduates. Haven was asked to deliver the philosophical oration. The general topic was determined by class standing and not necessarily a desire to speak about philosophy, but in retrospect, he was extremely well prepared for the task. He took as his title "The Identity of Philosophy," and while the vague description tells us little, the content of the speech made an impression.

Haven addressed the way mental powers were understood in that era. He echoed those who taught that people possess three distinct attributes: intelligence, sensibility (or feelings), and free will. This framework guided Luther Lee and was a central feature of Asa Mahan's teaching. Haven used

17. Prentice, *Life of Gilbert Haven,* 58–59.
18. Gravely, *Gilbert Haven Methodist Abolitionist,* 22.
19. Gravely, *Gilbert Haven Methodist Abolitionist,* 23–25.
20. *Declaration and Pledge against Slavery,* 1.

slightly different terminology. He named an intellectual, physical, and moral nature. Accordingly, the intellectual nature governed the intelligence and its perceptions of reality. The physical nature gave rise to desires of the sensibility. The moral nature expressed itself through free will and action. Haven insisted that these three dimensions of human personality were created for harmonious relationship with one another.[21]

The speech argued that history has witnessed ages when these faculties or powers were out of balance. Haven asserted that, at first, "the physical energies" dominated and drove people to violate "the higher principles of the reason and conscience."[22] Likewise, there have been times when the other two powers reigned. The oration ran to seven pages of handwritten text and never quite got out of the clouds. But we would be mistaken to write it off as an irrelevant head game. Less than five years later, Haven clarified his understanding of the mental faculties when arguing for obedience to God's law and against the Fugitive Slave provisions of 1850.

The Springs of Our Being

When most people think of Christian ministry, they imagine someone receiving a call that is then deepened through study and credentialing. It does not always happen this way. Some come to understand themselves and their vocation only after long and sustained reading, writing, conversation, and prayer. For these folks, ministry is not a clear task that finds resources through education. For them, ministry is who they are after a sustained journey of intellectual growth. Gilbert Haven was one such person.

Haven's commencement address regarding "The Identity of Philosophy" and its exploration of human nature was not an exercise in idle speculation so much as a consideration of how people are wired. It was also a vehicle for considering his own intellect, impulses, and moral commitments. He loved the life of the mind. It gave him a window on the self and helped him understand others.

Ten days following his graduation from Wesleyan University, Haven found himself teaching ancient languages at Amenia Seminary in Amenia, New York. According to tradition, the name "Amenia" means "a pleasant place."[23] Located some seventy miles west of Middletown, Con-

21. Haven, "Philosophical Oration," 1.
22. Haven, "Philosophical Oration," 1.
23. "Why Amenia."

necticut, the village was not far from the Hudson River Valley home of Sojourner Truth, but Haven and Truth became friends later, when they both lived in Massachusetts.

Amenia Seminary was a preparatory school, founded in 1835 by Methodists. Haven immersed himself in his work and pondered his vocation. Should he remain a teacher or move toward pastoral ministry? Two years into his employment at Amenia he was appointed principal of the institution. The job taxed his considerable energy but also gave him opportunities to develop a wide range of skills. He also met a young woman there named Mary Ingraham (1831–60). Over time Haven and Ingraham nurtured a bond that grew into a love story. They were married during 1851.

AMENIA SEMINARY AMENIA.

Amenia Seminary in Amenia, New York was the venue for Gilbert Haven's legendary sermon on "The Higher Law," November 1850.

Image Courtesy of Bill Jeffway, Dutchess County Historical Society, Poughkeepsie, New York

In 1849 Haven's hometown of Malden, Massachusetts, celebrated its bicentennial. He was summoned to write an epic poem for the occasion. The piece, some twenty pages long, extolled the New England virtues of independence, liberty, and civic responsibility. He wrote, "They are the pioneers in every cause, that aims to introduce God's perfect laws."[24] Soon he felt compelled to defend divine law in the face of oppressive human legislation.

When the so-called Compromise of 1850 made its Fugitive Slave provisions the law of the land, Haven responded with a groundbreaking sermon. This address, later published in a collection of sermons, speeches, and letters, established a trajectory for the rest of his life. It was delivered in Amenia during November of 1850—two months after the offending legislation had been signed by President Millard Filmore. Haven's use of language is telling. He referred to the act as the "Fugitive Slave Bill." Nothing so heinous could ever be properly considered law.

The sermon bore the title "The Higher Law" and granted that humanity is subject to public rules of conduct. However, the source and nature of these norms must be clearly understood. He argued that God, not political bodies, held ultimate authority and that people were created to live in harmony with a divine law. This law could be discovered through the various attributes of human personality, something Haven termed "the springs of our being."[25] What are these essential qualities? How should they work together? How are they designed to fulfill God's higher law?

Haven teased out the implications of his Wesleyan University philosophical oration. If people possess an intellectual nature (an intelligence), a physical nature (a sensibility), and a moral nature (free will), then these three must be created to help people keep God's law. By this time, he had advanced beyond a simple consideration of the faculties. Now he applied his philosophical analysis to moral obligation. Being must lead to ethical behavior.

Unlike others who spoke of the intellect, sensibility, and will, Haven often listed the sensibility first. Only then did he describe the intellect and the will. His sermon on "The Higher Law" put it this way: "These faculties are called generically the propensities or sensibilities, the intellect and the moral nature."[26] The order of the three was, for Haven, no accident. He claimed that the faculties related to one another in a distinct hierarchy.

24. *Bi-Centennial Book of Malden*, 79.
25. Haven, *National Sermons*, 1.
26. Haven, *National Sermons*, 3.

The sensibilities occupied the lowest position. The intellect held an elevated role. But the free will (or moral nature) reigned supreme.[27]

Tragically, according to Haven, humanity suffers from a pathological distortion of these faculties. The desires of the sensibilities cloud the intellect, and an impaired intellect cannot provide clarity for the will. Subsequently, people are often ruled by their self-serving motivations. In this fallen state, the world is ignorant of "the true law" or unable "to pursue it steadily."[28] All manner of private and public sin prevails, and Haven named slavery as one expression of this brokenness. Civil laws that sought to excuse slavery catered to the disordering of mental faculties. Such statutes failed to honor "the higher law of our nature," and they were to be resisted.[29]

Haven made his position clear: "When any human law is opposed to the evident decisions of divine law, those edicts are to be disobeyed both in what they command us to do, and in what they command us to refrain from doing."[30] Asa Mahan offered a similar argument following the Civil War: "To obey any law which prohibits what God commands, or commands what He prohibits, is treason toward God."[31] Haven had opened the door for civil disobedience, but it was a disobedience anchored in loyalty to divine law.

According to this perspective, even a reading of the United States Constitution requires discernment. When there is doubt regarding the various claims made upon citizens, "we must choose that which agrees best with the law written on our hearts."[32] Ultimately, God's law written on the heart grounded Haven's entire moral philosophy. This was an emphasis remarkably akin to the authenticity of Sojourner Truth's life. Saved by grace and freed to live, the internal compass of God's law directed her. It was Jer 31:33 all over again: "I will put my law within them, and I will write it on their hearts; and I will be their God, and they shall be my people" (NRSV). It is no wonder Haven and Truth understood each other so well.

The importance of Haven's 1850 sermon on "The Higher Law" cannot be overstated. Considered publicly, it was but one of many such addresses that autumn, but considered from a personal standpoint, it marked a

27. Haven, *National Sermons*, 4.

28. Haven, *National Sermons*, 5.

29. Haven, *National Sermons*, 6.

30. Haven, *National Sermons*, 23.

31. Mahan, *Misunderstood Texts of Scripture*, 162.

32. Haven, *National Sermons*, 28.

dramatic departure. William Gravely described this sermon as "the culmination of his vocational search and the inauguration of his distinctive mission in life."[33] Haven read, thought, wrote, and spoke to find his future, but in the end, it found him. He knew that he must answer the call. Therefore, as 1851 dawned, great changes were on the horizon.

By the spring of that year, Haven began pastoral ministry in Northampton, Massachusetts. He led a church there for two years before being moved to a different appointment. He next served in Wilbraham, then Westfield, Roxbury, and finally Cambridge.[34] Gilbert Haven and Mary Ingraham were married on September 17, 1851. Their partnership blazed bright for a little less than a decade before her tragic death.

Northampton was also the home of Sojourner Truth during the early and middle 1850s. The Havens and Truth began a friendship that would outlive Mary and last until Gilbert's death. As Margaret Washington observed, "Their egalitarian relationship puzzled even Haven's closest friends."[35] But their connection made perfect sense. Haven and Truth expressed the same love for God and respect for God's ways. They understood divine authority and lived it from the heart. Their friendship was as natural as the equality they embodied.

During the 1850s Haven tended to his duties and continued to preach about matters of justice. His star was rising, even as America careened toward Civil War. In 1869 he published a book of sermons, speeches, and letters on the abolitionist struggle. The "Higher Law" sermon led the collection. Many of these addresses were given in the same Massachusetts churches where he labored to preach the word, celebrate the sacraments, and order parish life. The title of the book signaled Haven's understanding of the Civil War. It speaks of slavery and "its war."[36] There was no equivocation. Others might describe the conflict as a clash over the prerogative of states, but Haven was having none of that. The war was about slavery, and any euphemistic attempts to explain it otherwise were disingenuous.

The introduction to this 1869 collection told a story, as well. Haven not only embraced his personal ministry; he also revered the tradition of New England clerical leadership. This movement had been a guiding force in early American life. New England divines excelled at "setting

33. Gravely, *Gilbert Haven Methodist Abolitionist*, 12.

34. Gravely, *Gilbert Haven Methodist Abolitionist*, 34.

35. Washington, *Sojourner Truth's America*, 268.

36. Haven, *National Sermons*.

forth the relations of the Gospel to the laws and customs of man."[37] Haven drew from this past and noted that "a sermon of Rev. Jonathan Mayhew of the West Church, Boston, on the Higher Law, by the confession of John Adams, was the opening gun of the Revolution."[38] Mayhew's sermon, published in 1750, argued that good human law was consistent with "the ordinances and commands of God."[39] When Haven celebrated the divine law, he did so as a son of New England.

Among the sermons in this collection was one preached two days before the Kansas-Nebraska Act received a presidential signature (May 30, 1854). Haven denounced the legislation in an address titled "The Death of Freedom." Always dramatic, he opened with these words: "We gather to-day around the corpse of Freedom."[40] He foresaw the bloodshed in Kansas and the irrepressible conflict that would follow.

Two years later Haven condemned a brutal attack on Senator Charles Sumner of Massachusetts in a sermon titled "The State Struck Down." Representative Preston Brooks, a proslavery ideologue from South Carolina, beat Sumner with a walking cane and left him unconscious in the Senate chamber. Sumner had made a name for himself as an outspoken abolitionist, and throughout the South many believed Brooks was merely defending their honor. Such vicious behavior shocked those in the North.

Haven concluded that the struggle over slavery had reached a point where "Right fell under the death-strokes of Might."[41] His language invoked a common aphorism, but it also revealed his philosophical approach to the law. Without a divine standard, human relations are reduced to raw power. There was such a thing as right, and it mattered.

The sermon condemning Brooks was preached in Westfield, Massachusetts, and before long another address from the same locale caught the eye of many. In November of 1856, James Buchanan was elected president of the United States. Haven feared that justice in America was imperiled as never before. He tried to remain hopeful but could not deny his despair. This sermon was titled "The National Midnight."

As war clouds became more ominous, many in the abolitionist movement put aside their differences to unite against slavery. Haven was

37. Haven, *National Sermons*, v.

38. Haven, *National Sermons*, vi.

39. Mayhew, *Discourse Concerning Unlimited Submission*, 18.

40. Haven, *National Sermons*, 33.

41. Haven, *National Sermons*, 65.

certainly willing to join hands with others for the cause, but he still insisted on political action. He praised William Lloyd Garrison in his sermon on the Kansas-Nebraska Act, but this did not mean he agreed with Garrison regarding methods for defeating slavery.[42] The two sparred right up to the opening of the Civil War.

In January of 1861, Garrison's *Liberator* published excerpts from a sermon Haven delivered the prior November, after Abraham Lincoln's election to the presidency. The sermon also included a critique of Garrison and his followers, charging them with unorthodox views that bordered on moral complacency: "Would that, in his sphere of effort, and to the measure of his large abilities and influence, he had kept his liberty from becoming licentiousness."[43] Perhaps Garrison had replaced proper devotion to God's higher law with outright antinomianism—hatred of law itself.

Garrison was not about to publish excerpts of this sermon without also printing a rebuttal. The rejoinder asked, "Who have advocated a more faithful adherence to principle, or a more uncompromising regard for the laws and commands of God, than ourselves?"[44] There was no real resolution to this debate. Within months the nation erupted in war, and the intramural squabble became irrelevant.

By all accounts, the marriage of Gilbert and Mary Haven exuded a tender authenticity. She was thoughtful, poised, and strong. He was genial, principled, and winsome, a magnet for those who appreciated good friendship. Mary Haven died on April 3, 1860, five days after giving birth to their fourth child. The babe was named Bertie and lived only three days following his mother's passing.[45]

Haven walked through grief the way most people do—with a mix of exhaustion and feeble attempts to project his old persona. But he was dying inside and needed a lifeline. Biographer George Prentice commented that "midnight gloom had settled down upon his pathway."[46] Yet at that precise moment "the national midnight" foreseen by Haven arrived in the form of Civil War. How would he respond to both crises?

42. Haven, *National Sermons*, 38.

43. Haven, "Anti-Slavery Struggle," 9.

44. "Sermons on the Times," 10.

45. Gravely, *Gilbert Haven Methodist Abolitionist*, 78.

46. Prentice, *Life of Gilbert Haven*, 193.

Gilbert Haven (1821–1880) understood the abolitionist movement to be
a fulfillment of the American revolutionary vision.

Image Courtesy of The General Commission on Archives and History,
The United Methodist Church

This War Begins in Our Moral Nature

Before sunrise on Friday, April 12, 1861, Confederate cannons opened fire
on Fort Sumter, Charleston, South Carolina. The long-anticipated war had
come. That spring Haven struggled under the weight of "overwork and a
broken heart."[47] He decided to collect himself and his energies in Malden.
However, he could not rest when President Lincoln issued a call for seventy-
five thousand volunteers to meet the Rebellion.

47. Daniels, *Memorials of Gilbert Haven*, 62.

Casual observers might assume that Haven simply rushed to enlist in the army as a massive wave of patriotism washed over the land. Military service offered him a chance to expedite the end of American slavery. There were, of course, elements of this motivation in his heart. But during April 1861 Haven embraced a distinctly melancholy mission. A letter of his reveals the truth: "The dreadful suffering in my soul had probably as much to do with my engaging in this service as the patriotic feeling."[48] He desired to shake off his grief, but he understood that this would only happen as he stepped forward and fulfilled his vocation. To find himself he had to be himself.

Haven wrote, "This sorrow and its accompanying weakness of body and spirit left me incapable of discharging my duties as a pastor. The Call of my Country and the sublime object to which it summoned me, seemed to be a providential summons."[49] On Thursday, April 18, 1861, he met Massachusetts Governor John Andrew and was referred to the Eighth Regiment of Volunteer Infantry. His commission as chaplain was sworn to the next day, April 19—the anniversary of the revolutionary battles at Lexington and Concord.[50] Everything he did was in sync with the rhythms of the American Revolution.

Haven published letters from the field during the war's first three months. Before the end of April, he was aboard a steamer off Annapolis, Maryland, and told of his first days in the service. The regiment had quartered at Boston's famed Faneuil Hall. He described bunking down on a straw mattress where, earlier, he had heard a host of luminaries speak—among them Daniel Webster, Theodore Parker, and Charles Sumner. The time for that kind of talk had ended. Now the nation needed action.[51]

He wrote from Camp Essex, Maryland, and prophesied the extinction of slavery. Then he penned a reflection regarding "Profit and Loss after Bull Run."[52] During the summer of 1861 the Union Army expected to thrash the enemy in northern Virginia. Instead, they were pushed from the field at Manassas (or Bull Run) on July 21. The war was not going to be won with pageantry and patriotic slogans. It demanded gritty persistence.

48. Letter from Gilbert Haven, Washington City, May 6, 1861, Monday, 9 a.m., in Haven, Papers.

49. Letter from Gilbert Haven, Washington City, May 6, 1861, Monday, 9 a.m., in Haven, Papers.

50. Letter from Gilbert Haven, Washington City, May 6, 1861, Monday, 9 a.m., in Haven, Papers.

51. Haven, National Sermons, 214–15.

52. Haven, National Sermons, 261–68.

The battle took place on a Sunday. The following Wednesday Haven composed himself and confronted the meaning of defeat. He began, "On a straw pallet, spread on a few rough, wet boards, lying loosely over the grassy ground, under leaky canvas, in the generally damp and sticky atmosphere of a tent in a shower, I am writing my last letter from the seat of war."[53] He blasted the pride that had led to disaster. He hoped that such bitter loss would weed out any remaining lethargy and unrealistic expectations. Then he turned to a metaphor that often appeared in his preaching: the revolutionary Battle of Bunker Hill.

This storied clash on June 17, 1775, was an American defeat, and yet it clarified commitment and demonstrated possibilities for victory. In 1861 Haven remarked that "the defeat at Bunker's Hill paved the way to the Declaration."[54] The spring and summer of 1775 led to the summer of 1776. Such trajectories are always clear in retrospect, but in the rain that soaked Maryland and Virginia during late July 1861, the future seemed less secure.

Haven did not re-enlist when his term of service ended. Instead, he once again returned to his Malden home. It grounded him and gave him space to reflect on his experience at the front. In October of 1861 he accepted a position as pastor of the Clinton Avenue Methodist Episcopal Church, Newark, New Jersey. This was a temporary appointment, and Haven planned to remain only until the following spring.

On April 30, 1862, he left from Boston to visit Europe. The trip may have been intended as a change of scenery to aid in his journey through grief. Perhaps some distance would offer perspective on his life and loss. The pilgrimage certainly put the American Civil War into worldwide perspective for him. Haven concluded that the conflict at home was about more than sectional animosities. It was a continuation of the uniquely American struggle between authoritarian and democratic government.

From Paris, on July 4, 1862, he wrote to the *London Watchman*, a Wesleyan publication. Haven attempted to interpret the Civil War for an English audience, and he did so by lauding the principles of American government. The first half of his letter was published, but it created a stir among the British public. The second half was withheld from the press.

During this period of the war, British society displayed an annoying sympathy for the American South. Haven explained this as a kinship with the

53. Haven, *National Sermons*, 261.

54. Haven, *National Sermons*, 267.

aristocratic culture that drove the Confederacy. Southern institutions mirrored the distinctions and exclusions still dominant in England. Union forces were fighting a mindset that placed nobility above ordinary people.

This interpretation implied that the Civil War was, in effect, a second movement of the American Revolution, and such a claim alienated British readers. Haven insisted, "Destroy distinctions in society; make the ruler subject to a written Constitution; choose him out of the people, to return in a brief time to the people; in a word, make the people sovereign, and armies and armaments will cease."[55] Others might have advanced a different argument, but Haven understood the Union cause as a fulfillment of America's appointed vocation to the world.

He returned to his homeland in early 1863 and assessed the strange fortunes of war. When he began his trip during the spring of 1862, things were looking up for the Union. Northern armies had largely recovered from their early reverses, and General George B. McClellan was mounting his Peninsula Campaign. After that effort stalled before Richmond, matters looked less promising, but the Union managed to salvage a technical victory at the Battle of Antietam in Sharpsburg, Maryland. This clash along Antietam Creek happened on Wednesday, September 17, 1862. The following Monday Abraham Lincoln issued his preliminary Emancipation Proclamation. It was due to take effect on January 1, 1863.

However, 1862 closed on a dire note for the nation. At Fredericksburg, Virginia, Confederate forces were dug in along a range of hills, and on December 13, Union General Ambrose Burnside threw thousands of men at the impregnable heights. It was murder from the start, and the Northern public recoiled at the slaughter. The new year came in with a decidedly mixed prognosis.

Haven had been lobbying for emancipation from the outset, and so he was buoyed in January 1863 when Lincoln's proclamation became established policy. Yet he understood that the war hung in the balance. The summer of 1863 brought the Battle of Gettysburg and the Union victory at Vicksburg, Mississippi, but there were defeats as well. Haven plumbed the depths of his tradition for wisdom and spoke about the war's higher purposes.

He identified the national mission with the advancement of human rights. He also saw this vocation as part of God's coming millennium. He preached several times regarding the hallowed call of America and near

55. Haven, *National Sermons*, 305.

the end of 1863 offered an address on "The War and the Millennium."[56] This sermon was grounded in Rev 17:14: "These shall make war with the Lamb, and the Lamb shall overcome them" (KJV). It was delivered following Union victories at Lookout Mountain and Missionary Ridge, near Chattanooga, Tennessee.

Haven defined the millennium as "the triumph of Christ over Satan in the hearts and lives, the laws and institutions, of man."[57] For him, the millennial reign of Christ was not really the achievement of powerful armies, and yet his rhetoric sometimes appeared to sanction violence as a means for creating the millennium. Was he simply one more religious zealot invoking righteousness to annihilate the enemy? There were moments when he stepped dangerously close to such reasoning.

However, Haven did his level best to articulate a theological definition of the millennium and a philosophical standard of right. Not surprisingly, he insisted that the reign of God begins in the human heart. More to the point, he emphasized the will as the seat of millennial awareness: "This war begins in our moral nature, and in the sovereign head of that nature, the free will."[58] From the will a proper ordering of faculties "extends through every emotion, sensibility, intellect, appetite, habit, custom, law, or institution, whether of the individual or society."[59] Some might conclude that Haven's understanding of the millennium simply celebrated militaristic triumph, but he understood the matter as a divine reclamation of the mental faculties.

By the time 1864 opened, there was cautious optimism that the northern armies would begin a series of victories. This was especially the case once General Ulysses S. Grant took command. Grant's Overland Campaign began in May and slogged it out with the Confederate Army along a line leading through the wilderness of Virginia's Spotsylvania County, Spotsylvania Court House, and other points on the way toward Richmond. Haven displayed a fondness for Grant. Later in life, he reportedly told a family member that the two greatest people in America were Ralph Waldo Emerson and Ulysses S. Grant.[60] On May 15, 1864, he preached a sermon on "Why Grant Will Succeed."

56. Haven, *National Sermons*, 373–92.
57. Haven, *National Sermons*, 374.
58. Haven, *National Sermons*, 374.
59. Haven, *National Sermons*, 374.
60. Prentice, *Life of Gilbert Haven*, 67–68.

Instead of emphasizing superior military power, supply, organization, and the application of force, Haven cast Grant's Overland Campaign
in moral terms. Prior to 1863 the Union Army of the Potomac had been
led by George McClellan, and McClellan demonstrated an aversion to the
abolitionist cause. He resisted identifying the Northern war effort with
emancipation. This, according to Haven, met with God's judgment. Only
an army devoted to true freedom and equality could carry the day.

Haven considered Grant more enlightened regarding the trajectory of
history and more open to using the military as an instrument for deliverance.
This did not mean that Haven always agreed with Grant, and later, when the
general was president, Haven reserved for himself a critical independence.
He insisted that "in estimating the reasons for our success, we shall ever bear
in mind that though great generals are a great necessity, great ideas are a
greater."[61] He never tired of emphasizing ideas over idols.

By July 4, 1864, the Union Army was settled into a siege outside of Pe-
tersburg, Virginia. The war still raged under a cloud of uncertainty, but Haven used the nation's birthday as an opportunity to revisit his favorite theme:
the relationship between the American Revolution and the current struggle.
His July 4 sermon bore the title "The Revolution and the Rebellion."

In many ways, this address extended the thinking of Haven's controversial essay on "England and America." The Civil War was, once again, cast
as a righteous cause. This claim found support in the parallels between the
Revolution and the current Rebellion. The comparison not only connected
the principles of both conflicts; it revealed similar experiences of trial and
triumph. Moreover, when compared with the American Revolution during
its third year, the Union effort of 1864 had even greater reason for hope.

Haven explained that the Revolution's third year offered little to inspire confidence: "A ragged, mutinous corps was all that were between
the country and its subjugation."[62] In contrast, the third year of fighting
during the Civil War brought great gains. The matter was not settled yet,
but light burned on the horizon. Just as the Declaration of Independence
faced uncertainty for several years before its ultimate vindication, Lincoln's Emancipation Proclamation could weather a time of challenge before its complete fruition.[63]

61. Haven, *National Sermons*, 397.
62. Haven, *National Sermons*, 409.
63. Haven, *National Sermons*, 411.

On April 9, 1865, Robert E. Lee's Army of Northern Virginia surrendered to Ulysses S. Grant's Army of the Potomac. Within days Haven preached a provocative sermon which compared Confederate president Jefferson Davis to the pharaoh of Exodus.[64] But time moved swiftly, and on April 14, Abraham Lincoln was assassinated.

The grief poured out of Haven. He delivered a memorial sermon on Sunday, April 23, bearing the title "The Uniter and Liberator of America." He compared the martyred president to Moses—a person of unsteady conviction who grew into an unyielding advocate for justice. Haven observed, "Men of ideas often fail when those ideas are born into actual life."[65] Not so with Abraham Lincoln; he was as good as his rhetoric.

Haven offered rare insight regarding the nature of Lincoln's devotion to worthy ideas. Instead of merely giving himself to abstractions such as "the nation" or "righteousness," Lincoln interpreted these notions through the dignity of persons: "He held every one in his heart of hearts; he felt a deep and individual regard for each and all."[66] During the same era, abolitionist philosopher Asa Mahan employed remarkably similar language when talking about the value of "each and all."[67]

After the war, Haven distinguished himself as a supporter of Reconstruction. From 1867 to 1872 he served as the editor of *Zion's Herald* in Boston, and in 1872 he was elected a bishop of the Methodist Episcopal Church. However, these worldly achievements could never match his fundamental commitment to human equality. In January of 1871 he joined his friend Sojourner Truth for a grand event marking the eighth anniversary of the Emancipation Proclamation. Gilbert Haven died in his beloved Malden on January 3, 1880. He is buried in the Salem Street Cemetery, Malden, Massachusetts.

We will probably never understand Haven's enthusiastic defense of John Brown, but we can appreciate that it grew out of his belief in a higher law beyond human authority. The claim may leave us unsettled, but for Gilbert Haven, complacency in matters of church and state was more dangerous than holy disobedience.

64. Haven, *National Sermons*, 529–50.

65. Haven, *National Sermons*, 556.

66. Haven, *National Sermons*, 561.

67. See Momany, *For Each and All*, 46.

EPILOGUE

To Think, to Feel,
to Act

A Movement Philosophy

ON CHRISTMAS DAY IN 1839, David Stedman Ingraham, a recent graduate of the Oberlin Collegiate Institute, visited Port Royal, Jamaica. Ingraham served as a missionary among recently freed people on the island. At Port Royal (near Kingston) he stepped aboard a ship that had been used to imprison and transport enslaved people from the west coast of Africa. The vessel, identified as the Portuguese brig *Ulysses*, was intercepted by the British war schooner *Skipjack* south of Cuba on November 30, 1839.

The people held captive on the *Ulysses* were released, and the ship was impounded. Ingraham boarded the ghostly craft and made a careful study of its condition. He followed his personal examination with a detailed letter to abolitionist newspapers. This letter, written on January 15, 1840, was directed toward youth, and Ingraham did not hold back when describing the sickening state of the vessel. He explained the oppressively tight quarters, the length of the brutal journey, and the filth where people were forced to lie. He closed the exposé with a call for action. Youngsters were urged to contemplate the horrors of the *Ulysses*, and "when they *think*, may they *feel*; and when they *feel*, may they *act*; and when they *act*, may God's blessing attend their efforts; and may the time soon come, when *slavery*, and all its attendant evils, shall curse our world no more."[1] Sadly, David Ingraham died of tuberculosis on August 1, 1841, the anniversary day of emancipation in the British West Indies.

1. Ingraham, "Capture of the Ulysses," 2.

136

Ingraham's summons to the youth of his time revealed a profound philosophical framework for change. The call to think, feel, and act mirrored the faculty psychology of many in the abolitionist movement. Harmonious relations between the intellect, the sensibility, and the will could transform the world. But where did Ingraham learn this grammar for justice?

As much as we might wish for a simple answer, the story is more complex. Ingraham graduated from Oberlin in 1837, and a look at the curriculum there is revealing. Among the required reading during 1836 was a tome on philosophy authored by the French thinker Victor Cousin, bearing the title *Elements of Psychology*.[2]

The book, translated in 1834 by American scholar Caleb Sprague Henry, was really a commentary on John Locke's classic work *An Essay Concerning Human Understanding* (1689). The tenth chapter of Cousin's text begins with an unwieldy statement:

> All the facts which can fall under the consciousness of man, and consequently under the reflection of the philosopher, resolve themselves into three fundamental facts, which contain all the others; three facts which, beyond doubt, are never, in reality, solitary and separate from each other, but which are essentially not the less distinct, and which a careful analysis ought to distinguish, without dividing, in the complex phenomenon of intellectual life. These three facts are expressed in the words: *to feel, to think, to act*.[3]

This word order resembled the description of human personality sometimes preferred by Gilbert Haven: the physical nature, the intellectual nature, and the moral nature. But the threefold pattern was clear.

Cousin's influence at Oberlin was pervasive and embraced by President Asa Mahan. Between 1835 and 1850 Mahan took this description of faculty psychology and made it a template for social action.

Mahan was born in central New York in 1799 and reared among a strict Presbyterian family. He attended Hamilton College in Clinton and was graduated from Andover Theological Seminary. His first formal parish appointment came near Rochester, New York, where he met young David Ingraham. A few years later Mahan settled with his family in Cincinnati, and by then his theological convictions had changed. Along the way he shifted from the Calvinist tradition and toward the Wesleyan emphasis

2. *Catalogue of the Trustees*, 22.
3. Cousin, *Elements of Psychology*, 245.

on graciously empowered free will.[4] Mahan, Ingraham, and many others headed to Oberlin in 1835.

Mahan appreciated the better characteristics of Enlightenment philosophy. He did not endorse those eighteenth-century thinkers who poured cold water on Christian conviction, but he happily employed certain Enlightenment ideas to explain the moral law. He believed that all people share a universal human nature. In 1846 Mahan wrote that all rights and interests of humanity "rest exclusively upon the permanent and changeless laws of human nature itself, upon the elements of humanity common to all individuals of the race."[5] He also believed that this shared identity is so sacred that any violation of its dignity in another degrades oneself.[6]

At root, Mahan parsed human nature according to categories of the mental faculties—the intellect, the sensibility, and the will. His 1839 *Scripture Doctrine of Christian Perfection* claimed that a sanctified intellect will seek "the truth and will of God, and by what means we may best meet the demands of the great law of love."[7] Likewise, the sensibility will be "in perfect and perpetual harmony with the truth and will of God as apprehended by the intellect."[8] The will of a sanctified person must be "in entire conformity to the will of God."[9] In sum, a mature person would see reality as God sees it, allow this truth to shape the feelings, and act according to the moral law.

In 1845 Mahan released two books that probed the mysteries of human nature. One, titled *A System of Intellectual Philosophy*, quoted Victor Cousin directly.[10] The other, *Doctrine of the Will*, addressed the relationship between all three mental faculties.

The eleventh chapter of the *Doctrine of the Will* presented a critical differentiation. Mahan examined the ordering of the faculties when action is right and the ordering of them when action is wrong. Accordingly, "In all acts and states morally right, the Will is in harmony with the Intelligence, from respect to moral obligation or duty; and all the desires and propensities, all the impulses of the Sensibility, are held in strict subordination."[11] As a contrast, "In all acts morally wrong, the Will is controlled by the

---

4. See Momany, *For Each and All*.

5. Mahan, "Certain Fundamental Principles," 228.

6. Mahan, "Certain Fundamental Principles," 229–30.

7. Mahan, *Scripture Doctrine of Christian Perfection*, 14.

8. Mahan, *Scripture Doctrine of Christian Perfection*, 15.

9. Mahan, *Scripture Doctrine of Christian Perfection*, 13.

10. Mahan, *System of Intellectual Philosophy*, 23.

11. Mahan, *Doctrine of the Will*, 156.

Sensibility, irrespective of the dictates of the Intelligence."[12] This explication might suggest that Mahan considered the intellect to be innately superior to the sensibility, but there was more to his approach.

By 1846 Mahan could say, "The great want of universal humanity is a knowledge of truth, and a state of feeling and action in harmony with truth manifested to the mind."[13] The emphasis on "truth" reflected Mahan's devotion to the Scottish philosophy of Common Sense. This popular perspective claimed that the world around us could be known with some objective certainty. For Mahan, there was no moral value without truth. It is no wonder that David Ingraham, a recent Oberlin graduate, implored the young readers of his January 1840 letter to develop critical thinking, compassionate feeling, and just action.

Asa Mahan (1799–1889) provided an intellectual grounding for many abolitionists.

Image Courtesy of Shipman Library, Adrian College

12. Mahan, *Doctrine of the Will*, 156.
13. Mahan, "Certain Fundamental Principles," 234.

Common Threads

Asa Mahan's thought lurks among the shadows of the five abolitionists featured in this book. Mahan and Sojourner Truth both lived in southern Michigan during the later 1850s and 1860s, though they probably never met. Yet Truth's life terminated in something akin to Mahan's "evangelical spirit." Mahan and Luther Lee were both born in the revival regions of New York State, and they worked together at Adrian College during the Civil War. Moreover, Lee quoted directly from Mahan's *Doctrine of the Will* when writing his *Elements of Theology* (1856).[14]

Mahan and Laura Haviland both lived in Adrian, Michigan, after the late 1850s and were partners in advocacy on behalf of orphaned children following the Civil War. It is unknown if Henry Bibb ever met Asa Mahan, but a beloved copy of Bibb's *Narrative*, from Mahan's personal library, is stored in the United Methodist archives at Adrian College. Additionally, Bibb's claim that "consistent action is the key to emancipation" dovetails perfectly with the faculty psychology of that era.[15] Gilbert Haven was considerably younger than Mahan and did not reside in Michigan, but he read Mahan's *Scripture Doctrine of Christian Perfection* at an early point in his ministry.[16]

In 1883 Mahan released a two-volume study that stood as his crowning work: *A Critical History of Philosophy*. Within its pages he sorted the history of thought into four dominant approaches to reality: Skepticism, Materialism, Idealism, and Realism.

Skepticism embraced one stream of the Enlightenment and argued that people can never know ultimate reality for certain. Materialism posited that the very nature of reality is nothing more than the sum of physical, biological, and chemical processes. Idealism resisted Materialism and claimed that higher truths, beyond simple actions and reactions, guide the world. Realism appreciated the emphasis on higher truths but grounded them in knowable facts. Asa Mahan was a self-avowed Realist.[17]

During the nineteenth century, Skepticism dominated various parts of America, but the other three views tended to thrive in specific regions. Materialism took hold in the South, especially among the medical sciences, and this view sometimes made racist distinctions between people. Idealism

14. Lee, *Elements of Theology*, 186.

15. Bibb, "Consistency Is a Gem," 93.

16. Prentice, *Life of Gilbert Haven*, 43.

17. Mahan, *Critical History of Philosophy*.

ruled the Northeast—particularly the area around Boston. It was identified with many in the abolitionist movement, but it celebrated theories that were sometimes untethered from tangible practice. Realism held sway in the Mid-Atlantic states and then migrated westward throughout the Old Northwest. While considered uninspired by most later observers, Realism did offer a connection between theory and action.[18]

As the twentieth century opened, Realism became associated with musty convictions that failed to keep pace with the times. Thinkers questioned whether ultimate reality could be known with such confidence. The critique was often presented as a coming of age and an arrival at more sophisticated conclusions. However, this new vantage point also gave cover for those who were completely uninterested in questions of truth. The twentieth century—and its supposed sophistication—witnessed world cataclysm and brutality on an unprecedented scale. Perhaps the unrestrained destruction had origins in a disregard for the truth of things. After all, if there is no truth, then raw power determines acceptable action. Predators thrive in such environments.

Asa Mahan spent his later years in England, leading various revival programs. He died on April 4, 1889, and is buried in Ocklynge Cemetery, Eastbourne. When he left the world, a profoundly philosophical grounding for Christian social action was buried with him.

Finding Our Equilibrium

Among the Methodist abolitionists considered in this book, Gilbert Haven embodied the best developed faculty psychology. From the esoteric musings of his 1846 commencement oration to his later consideration of the millennium, the relationship between the intellect, the sensibility, and the will permeated his writing. Haven's 1863 longing for the millennium united the authority of God with properly ordered faculties: "The perfected deliverance is the Millennium. It is God again at the helm of the soul, voluntarily restored there as He was voluntarily expelled; God moving thence through every thought, impulse, volition, bringing all into subjection to Him."[19] Every thought, impulse, volition. Here was the higher law, once again honored by harmonious mental faculties.

18. Riley, *American Philosophy*, 3–22.
19. Haven, *National Sermons*, 375.

To describe the lives of the five people we have profiled as "compelling" means something. They are certainly captivating, but more is implied than simple interest in their stories. Most definitions of the term "compelling" describe a power to evoke admiration. This is, of course, true of these five witnesses. They are inviting examples and inspiring role models. But even this description of their significance is, at best, imprecise.

When we say that the five are compelling, we suggest that they communicate a responsibility for us. They ask us to be and do something. Eventually, we must consider ways to carry their legacy.

The interlocking ideas that inspired these abolitionists are also available to us today. The notion of a higher law, the inclusive redemption of Jesus Christ, the power to live God's way by grace, the critical importance of voice and agency—all these and more are as real now as they were before the Civil War. Some of their ideas offer a specific approach for understanding our very selves and our vocation.

The inheritance received from the faculty psychology tradition is one example. We do not have to define ourselves rigidly by nineteenth-century categories, but we can appreciate the strengths of a philosophy that stresses thought, feeling, and action. David Ingraham reminds us that transforming injustice requires a willingness to face the truth. Opening our minds to the way things are, allowing the truth to move our sensibilities, and then acting freely on behalf of others strikes me as a refreshing, even elegant, way to live the gospel. This is no arcane game, either. Those who dismiss philosophical ideas might remember that the destiny of faculty psychology is action!

Still, the concern for truth is not limited to confronting facts and honoring the realities around us. There is a primary celebration of truth required by those who follow Christ. That truth can be summed up by the life, death, and resurrection of Jesus. Asa Mahan and others taught that the created worth of people demanded a respect for the value of each human being. However, in Mahan's view, the greatest affirmation of personal worth came through the atonement offered by Christ.

He outlined three approaches to the atonement of Jesus. First, there was the teaching of limited atonement. According to this view Christ died for an elect group of people. Mahan was no fan of limited atonement. Second, there was the approach of general atonement. According to this view Jesus died for all people but for no one in particular. This perspective was widely accepted in Wesleyan circles, and Mahan considered it to be more correct than limited atonement. Yet he still found it inadequate.[20]

Finally, there was the view that instead of dying for no one in particular, Christ died for every human being in a personal and specific way. Mahan drew from Heb 2:9 when making this argument. He wrote, "The redemption of Christ had as special a regard to each individual, as if that one individual was alone concerned in it."[21] However, this intensely personal affirmation was not really a private possession. It was a truth expressed for every person on earth, and such an understanding of the atonement grounded Mahan's entire approach to human dignity. He termed it "special redemption" or "special atonement." While acknowledging the created value of people, his theological genius highlighted the redeemed value of all declared by Christ.[22]

This emphasis on both created and redeemed value was embodied by the five Methodists we have studied. Some were more explicit than others. For instance, Henry Bibb's concern for voice and human agency was all about personal value, but he worked through these matters in oblique, literary ways. Laura Haviland, on the other hand, spoke of both a created value held by all people and a redeemed value affirmed by the life, death, and resurrection of Jesus. She repeatedly emphasized the sacrificial death of Jesus for each and all in her attack on slavery.

Sojourner Truth knew herself to be reclaimed by Christ and given new life, but she began to live in earnest when her redemption was reflected outward through a love for every human being. Luther Lee also believed that the atonement offered by Jesus extended to all. Not surprisingly, he too relied upon Heb 2:9: "That he, by the grace of God, should taste death for every man (KJV)."[23] This expansive view of the atonement meant that every single human being must be treated with respect.

When these five oriented their thought, feeling, and action to this truth, they were unstoppable. Not only did they receive personal affirmation this way; they found the gracious ability to affirm others. For instance, Gilbert Haven's elaborate concern for properly ordered mental faculties stood in desperate need of grace. The free will may have been designed

20. Mahan, *Scripture Doctrine of Christian Perfection*, 153–54.

21. Mahan, *Scripture Doctrine of Christian Perfection*, 154.

22. On created value, which Mahan termed "intrinsic worth," see especially *Science of Moral Philosophy*, 81, 85–86, and 223; *Doctrine of the Will*, 163.

23. Lee, *Elements of Theology*, 146.

by God as an arbiter between the sensibility and the intellect, but natural willpower cannot guarantee authentic living.

Asa Mahan insisted that honoring God's law was never a matter of relying on "our own natural powers as moral agents, but upon the provisions of divine grace."[24] This was the same grace that affirmed the worth of all people. The five Methodists profiled in this study deserve admiration for many reasons, but perhaps most significant is the way they opened themselves to grace and lived a moral law that recognized the value of every person.

24. Mahan, *Scripture Doctrine of Christian Perfection*, 213.

BIBLIOGRAPHY

"The Annual Report of the American and Foreign Anti-Slavery Society, Presented at New-York, May 6, 1851; with the Addresses and Resolutions." New York: William Harned, 1851.

Armstrong, Douglas V., and LouAnn Wurst. "Clay Faces in an Abolitionist Church: The Wesleyan Methodist Church in Syracuse, New York." *Historical Archaeology* 37:2 (2003) 19–37.

"The Aunt Laura Haviland Memorial Fountain Unveiled." *Adrian Daily Telegram*, June 24, 1909.

Baker, Frank. "The Origins, Character, and Influence of John Wesley's Thoughts upon Slavery." *Methodist History* 22 (Jan 1984) 75–86.

Bibb, Henry. "Consistency Is a Gem." *The Signal of Liberty*, October 3, 1846.

———."Is the M. E. Church of the North Pro-Slavery?" *Voice of the Fugitive*, June 18, 1851.

———. Letter to the Editor. *The Liberator*, June 25, 1847.

———. *Narrative of the Life and Adventures of Henry Bibb, An American Slave, Written by Himself with an Introduction by Lucius C. Matlack*. New York: Published by the author, 1849.

The Bi-Centennial Book of Malden. Containing the Oration and Poem Delivered on the Two Hundredth Anniversary of the Incorporation of the Town, May 23, 1849; With Other Proceedings on That Day; and Matters Pertaining to the History of the Place. Boston: Geo. C. Rand, 1850.

Birney, James G. *American Churches, the Bulwarks of American Slavery*. 3rd American ed. Newburyport, MA: Charles Whipple, 1842.

Blackstone, William. *Commentaries on the Laws of England, Book the First*. Oxford: Clarendon, 1768.

———. *Commentaries on the Laws of England: A Facsimile of the First Edition of 1765–1769*. Vol. 1. Chicago: University of Chicago Press, 1979.

———. *Commentaries on the Laws of England, In Four Books: Book One*. Portland, Maine: Thomas B. Wait, 1807.

Blackwell, Robert Emory. "Smith, William Andrew (November 29, 1802–March 1, 1870)." In *Dictionary of American Biography*, 17:361–62. New York: Charles Scribner's Sons, 1943.

Bryant Lowe, Berenice. Papers: 1880s–1980s, box 1, folder 9, Michigan Historical Collections. Bentley Historical Library.

Buckley, Nick. "The Rise and Fall of Harmonia, a Spiritualist Utopia and Home to Sojourner Truth." *Battle Creek Enquirer*, January 16, 2019.

Capers, William, ed. *Southern Christian Advocate*. March 9, 1838.

Carter, George Edward. "The Use of the Doctrine of Higher Law in the American Anti-Slavery Crusade, 1830–1860." PhD diss., University of Oregon, 1970.

Catalogue of the Trustees, Officers, & Students of the Oberlin Collegiate Institute, Oberlin, 1836. Cleveland: F. B. Penniman, 1836.

Coke, Thomas, and Francis Asbury, eds. *Minutes of Several Conversations between the Rev. Thomas Coke, LLD., the Rev. Francis Asbury and Others, at a Conference, Begun in Baltimore, in the State of Maryland, on Monday, the 27th. of December, in the Year 1784. Composing a Form of Discipline for the Ministers, Preachers and Other Members of the Methodist Episcopal Church in America*. Philadelphia: Charles Cist, 1785.

Cooper, Afua Ava Pamela. "'Doing Battle in Freedom's Cause': Henry Bibb, Abolitionism, Race Uplift, and Black Manhood, 1842–1854." PhD diss., University of Toronto, 2000.

Cousin, Victor. *Elements of Psychology: Included in a Critical Examination of Locke's Essay on the Human Understanding*. Translated by C. S. Henry. Hartford: Cooke, 1834.

Cross, Whitney R. *The Burned-Over District: The Social and Intellectual History of Enthusiastic Religion in Western New York, 1800–1850*. Ithaca: Cornell University Press, 1950.

Daniels, W. H., ed. *Memorials of Gilbert Haven, Bishop of the Methodist Episcopal Church*. With an introduction by Bradford K. Peirce, D. D. Boston: B. B. Russell, 1880.

Dann, Norman K. *Practical Dreamer: Gerrit Smith and the Crusade for Social Reform*. Hamilton, NY: Log Cabin, 2009.

Dayton, Donald W. *Discovering an Evangelical Heritage*. New York: Harper and Row, 1976.

The Declaration and Pledge against Slavery, Adopted by the Religious Anti-Slavery Convention, Held at the Marlboro' Chapel, Boston, February 26, 1846. Boston: Devereux and Seaman, 1846.

Douglass, Frederick. *My Bondage and My Freedom*. In *Frederick Douglass Autobiographies*. New York: Library of America, 1994.

Dumond, Dwight L., ed. *Letters of James Gillespie Birney: 1831–1857*. 2 vols. New York: D. Appleton-Century, 1938.

Emerson, Michael O., and Christian Smith. *Divided by Faith: Evangelical Religion and the Problem of Race in America*. Oxford: Oxford University Press, 2000.

Fairbank, Calvin. *Rev. Calvin Fairbank during Slavery Times*. Chicago: R. R. McCabe, 1890.

Field, David N. "Imaging the 'Exotic Other': John Wesley and the People of Africa." *Wesley and Methodist Studies* 15:1 (2023) 64–75.

Filler, Louis. *The Crusade against Slavery, 1830–1860*. New York: Harper and Brothers, 1960.

"First Annual Commencement of Adrian College." *Adrian Daily Expositor*, June 13, 1860.

"The Fugitive Burned." *The Liberator*, October 28, 1853.

"Fugitive Slaves in Canada West." *Voice of the Fugitive*, January 1, 1851.

Fulwood, Sam III. "Black, White Feminists Are Caught Up in Monumental Scrap." *Los Angeles Times*, April 1, 1997.

Gerson, Michael. "What One of the Founders of Evangelicalism Can Teach Us about Racism." *Washington Post*, June 15, 2020.

Gravely, William B. *Gilbert Haven Methodist Abolitionist: A Study in Race, Religion, and Reform, 1850–1880.* Nashville: Abingdon, 1973.

Green, Michael S. *Politics and America in Crisis: The Coming of the Civil War.* Santa Barbara, CA: Praeger, 2010.

Gurney, Joseph John. *Letter to Friends of the Monthly Meeting of Adrian, Michigan.* New York: Mahlon Day, 1839.

Hamilton, Alexander. *The Farmer Refuted: or, A More Impartial and Comprehensive View of the Dispute between Great-Britain and the Colonies, Intended as a Further Vindication of the Congress: In Answer to a Letter from A. W. Farmer, Intitled A View of the Controversy between Great-Britain and Her Colonies: Including a Mode of Determining the Present Disputes Finally and Effectually, &c.* New York: James Rivington, 1775.

Haven, Gilbert. "The Anti-Slavery Struggle." *The Liberator,* January 18, 1861.

———. *National Sermons. Sermons, Speeches and Letters on Slavery and Its War: From the Passage of the Fugitive Slave Bill to the Election of President Grant.* Boston: Lee and Shepard, 1869.

———. Papers. United Methodist Church Archives, GCAH, Madison, NJ.

———. "Philosophical Oration: The Identity of Philosophy." Commencement, Wesleyan University, August 5, 1846. Wesleyan University, Special Collections and Archives.

Haviland, Laura. "March 1, 1890." Diary. Lenawee Historical Society Museum.

———. "A Story of Slavery and Deliverance." *Adrian Daily Expositor,* August 10, 1860.

———. *A Woman's Life-Work: Labors and Experiences.* Cincinnati: Walden and Stowe, 1882.

———. *A Woman's Life-Work: Labors and Experiences.* Chicago: C. V. Waite, 1887.

Hoare, Prince. *Memoirs of Granville Sharp, Esq. Composed from His Own Manuscripts, and Other Authentic Documents in the Possession of His Family and of the African Institution.* London: Henry Colburn, 1820.

Hood, J. W. *One Hundred Years of the African Methodist Episcopal Zion Church; or, The Centennial of African Methodism.* New York: A. M. E. Zion Book Concern, 1895.

Hosmer, William. *The Higher Law, in Its Relations to Civil Government: With Particular Reference to Slavery, and the Fugitive Slave Law.* Auburn, NY: Derby and Miller, 1852.

Hynson, Leon O. "Wesley's 'Thoughts upon Slavery': A Declaration of Human Rights." *Methodist History* 33:1 (Oct 1994) 46–57.

Ingraham, David. "Capture of the Ulysses—Sufferings of the Slaves." *The Colored American,* April 4, 1840.

"Just Published." *The Liberator,* April 26, 1850.

Kaufman, Paul Leslie. *"Logical" Luther Lee and the Methodist War against Slavery.* Lanham, MD: Scarecrow, 2000.

Lee, Luther. *Autobiography of the Rev. Luther Lee, D.D.* New York: Phillips and Hunt, 1882.

———. *Elements of Theology, or an Exposition of the Divine Origin, Doctrines, Morals and Institutions of Christianity.* Syracuse: Samuel Lee, 1856.

———. *Five Sermons and a Tract.* Edited by Donald W. Dayton. Chicago: Holrad House, 1975.

———. "Fourth of July Oration." *The Liberator,* August 3, 1860.

———. "The Fugitive Slave Law: Its Unconstitutionality." *The True Wesleyan,* 8:43, October 26, 1850.

———. "The Fugitive Slave Law: Its Unconstitutionality." *The True Wesleyan,* 8:44, November 2, 1850.

———. "The Fugitive Slave Law: Its Unconstitutionality." *The True Wesleyan*, 8:45, November 9, 1850.

———. *Slavery Examined in the Light of the Bible.* Syracuse: Wesleyan Methodist Book Room, 1855.

Lewis, Amy. "Who'll Speak for Malinda? Alternate Narratives of Freedom in *The Life and Adventures of Henry Bibb*." *African American Review* 52:3 (Fall 2019) 255–76.

Mahan, Asa. "Certain Fundamental Principles, Together with Their Applications." *Oberlin Quarterly Review* 35 (Nov 1846) 227–43.

———. *A Critical History of Philosophy.* 2 Vols. London: Elliot Stock, 1883.

———. *Doctrine of the Will.* New York: Mark H. Newman, 1845.

———. *Misunderstood Texts of Scripture Explained and Elucidated, and the Doctrine of the Higher Life Thereby Verified.* London: Salvation Army, 1876.

———. *Science of Moral Philosophy.* Oberlin: James M. Fitch, 1848.

———. *Scripture Doctrine of Christian Perfection; With Other Kindred Subjects, Illustrated and Confirmed in a Series of Discourses Designed to Throw Light on the Way of Holiness.* Boston: D. S. King, 1839.

———. *A System of Intellectual Philosophy.* New York: Saxton and Miles, 1845.

Malcom, Rudy. "Does the Sojourner Truth Project Uphold Its Own Mission?" *Scribbling Women*, Mar 6, 2020. https://literaryarchive.net/2020/03/06/does-the-sojourner-truth-project-uphold-its-own-mission/.

Mathews, Alfred. *History of Cass County, Michigan, with Illustrations and Biographical Sketches of Some of Its Prominent Men and Pioneers.* Chicago: Waterman, Watkins, 1882.

Mathews, Donald G. *Slavery and Methodism: A Chapter in American Morality, 1780–1845.* Princeton: Princeton University Press, 1965.

Matlack, Lucius C. *The Life of Rev. Orange Scott: Compiled from His Personal Narrative, Correspondence, and Other Authentic Sources of Information.* New York: C. Prindle and L. C. Matlack, 1847.

Mayhew, Jonathan. *A Discourse Concerning Unlimited Submission and Non-Resistance to the Higher Powers: With Some Reflections on the Resistance Made to King Charles I. And on the Anniversary of His Death.* Boston: D. Fowle and D. Gookin, 1750.

McKeon, Richard, ed. *Introduction to Aristotle.* 2nd ed. Chicago: University of Chicago Press, 1973.

Minutes of the South Carolina Conference of the Methodist Episcopal Church, for the Year 1836. Charleston: J. S. Burges, 1836.

Momany, Christopher P. *For Each and All: The Moral Witness of Asa Mahan.* Nashville: Wesley's Foundery, 2018.

Moore, William, and Jane Ann Moore, eds. *His Brother's Blood: Speeches and Writings, 1838–64.* Urbana, IL: University of Illinois Press, 2004.

Morrison, Toni. "The Site of Memory." In *Inventing the Truth: The Art and Craft of Memoir*, edited by William Zinsser, 2nd ed., 83–102. Boston: Houghton Mifflin, 1995.

Morton, Nelle. "Beloved Image: Feminist Imagining: Seeing and Hearing A-new." Unpublished manuscript, American Academy of Religion, December 28, 1977. Nelle Morton Archives, Presbyterian History Center, Montreat, NC.

"Mr. Bibb's Lectures." *The Signal of Liberty*, October 21, 1844.

Mull, Carol E. *The Underground Railroad in Michigan.* Jefferson, NC: McFarland, 2010.

Niebuhr, H. Richard. *The Kingdom of God in America.* New York: Harper and Brothers, 1937.

Norwood, Frederick A. *The Story of American Methodism.* Nashville: Abingdon, 1974.

Parker, Theodore. *A Letter to the People of the United States Touching the Matter of Slavery.* Boston: James Munroe, 1848.

Patterson, L. Dale. "Discovery." *Methodist History* 51:3 (Apr 2013) 233–36.

Paul, Nathaniel. *An Address, Delivered on the Celebration of the Abolition of Slavery, in the State of New York, July 5, 1827.* Albany: John E. Van Steenbergh, 1827.

Phoebus, George A., ed. *Beams of Light on Early Methodism in America: Chiefly Drawn from the Diary, Letters, Manuscripts, Documents, and Original Tracts of the Rev. Ezekiel Cooper.* New York: Phillips and Hunt, 1887.

Prentice, George. *The Life of Gilbert Haven, Bishop of the Methodist Episcopal Church.* New York: Phillips and Hunt, 1883.

Prest, Wilfrid. "Blackstone, Sir William (1723–1780)." In *Oxford Dictionary of National Biography*, 6:10–17. Oxford: Oxford University Press, 2004.

"Proceedings of the Annual Meeting of the Friends of Human Progress in Michigan." *The Anti-Slavery Bugle*, November 8, 1856.

Redpath, James. *Echoes of Harper's Ferry.* Boston: Thayer and Eldridge, 1860.

Riley, I. Woodbridge. *American Philosophy: The Early Schools.* New York: Dodd, Mead and Company, 1907.

Roosevelt, Eleanor, et al. *Universal Declaration of Human Rights.* New York: UN General Assembly, December 10, 1948.

Sandburg, Carl. *Abraham Lincoln: The War Years.* Vol. 2. New York: Harcourt, Brace and World, 1939.

"Sermons on the Times." *The Liberator*, January 18, 1861.

Seward, William H. *Speech of William H. Seward, on the Admission of California. Delivered in the Senate of the United States, March 11, 1850.* Washington, DC: Buell and Blanchard, 1850.

Sharp, Granville. *A Representation of the Injustice and Dangerous Tendency of Tolerating Slavery; or of Admitting the Least Claim of Private Property in the Persons of Men, in England.* London: Benjamin White, 1769.

Smith, Harmon, L. "William Capers and William A. Smith: Neglected Advocates of the Pro-Slavery Moral Argument." *Methodist History* (Oct 1964) 23–32.

Smith, Warren Thomas. *John Wesley and Slavery.* Nashville: Abingdon, 1986.

Smith, William A. *Lectures on the Philosophy and Practice of Slavery, as Exhibited in the Institution of Domestic Slavery in the United States: With the Duties of Masters to Slaves.* Edited by Thomas O. Summers, D.D. Nashville: Stevenson and Evans, 1856.

Somerset v. Stewart. *Howell's State Trials*, vol. 20, 1–82. London: Hansard, 1814.

Stilwell, R. L. "Rev. William Hosmer." *Twenty-Second Annual Session of the Central New York Conference of the Methodist Episcopal Church, Held October 9th to 15th, 1889, Watkins, N. Y.* Ithaca, NY: Journal Book and Commercial Printing House, 1889.

"Stop #16: Sojourner Truth's House." Sojourner Truth Memorial Committee. https://sojournertruthmemorial.org/walking-tour-map/thirty-five-park-street/.

"To Our Readers." *Voice of the Fugitive*, December 17, 1851.

Truth, Sojourner. *Narrative of Sojourner Truth; A Bondswoman of Olden Time, Emancipated by the New York Legislature in the Early Part of the Present Century; with a History of Her Labors and Correspondence Drawn from Her "Book of Life."* Battle Creek, MI: Published for the author, 1881.

———. *Narrative of Sojourner Truth, a Northern Slave, Emancipated from Bodily Servitude by the State of New York, in 1828.* Boston: Printed for the author, 1850.

———. "Truth, Sojourner, to Amy Kirby Post." October 1, 1865. RBSCP Exhibits. https://rbscpexhibits.lib.rochester.edu/items/show/3798.

Tucker, Veta Smith. *A Twenty-First Century History of the 1847 Kentucky Raid into Cass County, Michigan.* Kalamazoo, MI: Fortitude, 2010.

Washington, Margaret. *Sojourner Truth's America.* Urbana, IL: University of Illinois Press, 2009.

Wesley, John. "A Calm Address to Our American Colonies." In *The Works of John Wesley*, edited by Thomas Jackson. Vol. 11, *Thoughts, Addresses, Prayers, Letters*, 80–90. Grand Rapids: Baker, 1986.

———. "Letter to a Friend." In *The Works of John Wesley*, edited by Thomas Jackson. Vol. 13, *Letters*, 153. Grand Rapids: Baker, 1986.

———. "Letter to the Gentleman's Magazine." In *The Works of John Wesley*, edited by Thomas Jackson. Vol. 14, *Grammars, Musical Works, Letters, Indexes*, 360–61. Grand Rapids: Baker, 1986.

———. "Letters to Robert C. Brackenbury, Esq." In *The Works of John Wesley*, edited by Thomas Jackson. Vol. 13, *Letters*, 9. Grand Rapids: Baker, 1986.

———. "Thoughts upon Slavery." In *The Works of John Wesley*, edited by Thomas Jackson. Vol. 11, *Thoughts, Addresses, Prayers, Letters*, 59–79. Grand Rapids: Baker, 1986.

———. *The Works of John Wesley*, edited by Albert C. Outler. Vol. 1, *Sermons I*, 1–33, Nashville: Abingdon, 1984.

"Why Amenia." Amenia Historical Society. https://ameniahs.org/portfolio/our-name/.

Wiecek, William M. *The Sources of Antislavery Constitutionalism in America, 1760–1848.* Ithaca: Cornell University Press, 1977.

Made in United States
Troutdale, OR
08/09/2023

11944388R00105